THE BUSINESS PLAN

A State-of-the-Art Guide

Michael O'Donnell

LORD
PUBLISHING

Lord Publishing, Inc.
P.O. Box 806
Dover, Massachusetts
02030

Lord Publishing, Inc.

P.O. 806

Dover, MA 02030

(508) 785-0666

Lord Publishing, Inc. is a twelve-year old company dedicated to providing books, software, case studies and other business tools to entrepreneurs. The company has developed the first of a family of personal computer software products designed exclusively for the needs of new and growing ventures.

Ronstadt's FINANCIALS is a trademark of Lord Publishing, Inc.

IBM PC, XT, AT and PC-DOS are registered trademarks of International Business Machines Corp. MS-DOS is a registered trademark of Microsoft Corporation.

ISBN 0-930204-26-3

Dedicated to you — The Entrepreneur.

You are among a rare and inspiring breed
of individuals who are redefining the way
America lives and works.

LORD PUBLISHING, INC., 1988

Contents

Acknowledgements

Many important people took time from their busy schedules to review the first draft of this guide. They offered a lot of insights into the trials and tribulations of starting a new business. Looking over the list, you will find they make up an impressive group of professionals, representing all areas of business disciplines. We gratefully acknowledge their assistance.

Doug Betlach — Small Business Management Coordinator, North Valley Vocational Center

Leonard Christianson — Technical Director, Center for Innovation

Leon F. Dubourt — Chairman of the Board, Walhalla State Bank

Michael J. Gallagher — Business Development Specialist, U.S. Small Business Administration

Jon Geyerman — President, Norman Jessen and Associates, Inc.

Bruce Gjovig — Director, Center for Innovation and Business Development

Marv Kaiser — Attorney-at-Law

Patrick Marx — Minnesota World Trade Center

Robert W. Nelson — President, Grand Forks Development Foundation

Garry A. Pearson — Pearson and Christensen, Attorneys-at-Law

Tom Rolfstad — Economic Development Planner, North Dakota Economic Development Commission

Bill Schott — Development Coordinator, Basin Electric Corporation

Lyle C. Sorum — Vice President, Director of Marketing, Bremer Financial Service, Inc.

Dave Stenseth — President, Sioux Falls Development Corporation

Reed A. Stigen — CPA, Charles Bailly and Company

Chuck Stroup — Vice President, Union State Bank

Jerry Udell, Ph.D. — Professor of Marketing, Minutemen Graduate Program, UND

Richard Wold — President, First National Bank

Special thanks to Sandy Kovar, for her patience and dedication in typing the many drafts.

About the Author

Michael O'Donnell
Author

Michael O'Donnell is a Business Consultant with the Promersberger Company in Fargo, North Dakota, specializing in marketing plan development for the firm's clients. Previous to joining the "P" Company, he worked on the staff of the Center for Innovation and Business Development at the University of North Dakota, where he worked with inventors and entrepreneurs on a daily basis. Mr. O'Donnell is also the Founder and President of ASK-ME Systems, Incorporated, a manufacturer and distributor of public access videotex systems. Mr. O'Donnell has started six businesses of his own and has consulted with over sixty start-up projects. He serves on the faculty of the Commercialization Planning Workshop for the National Energy-Related Inventions Program. In this capacity he provides business plan and marketing plan assistance to some of the country's top inventors.

Bruce Gjovig
Senior Editor

Bruce Gjovig is a Business Consultant and Founding Director of the Center for Innovation and Business Development at the University of North Dakota. The Center for Innovation has been actively involved in scores of business start-ups or product introductions, and Mr. Gjovig has been strategically involved in most of those entrepreneurial ventures. The Center is receiving national attention for their programs and for their success in technology transfer. Mr. Gjovig is known as a champion for inventors, entrepreneurs, and venture capital causes in the Upper Midwest, and sponsored and helped found the First Seed Capital Group, the North Dakota Venture Capital Fund, and North Dakota Inventors Congress, the North Dakota Entrepreneur Hall of Fame, High School Entrepreneurs Clubs, and UND Chapter of the Association of Collegiate Entrepreneurs, the national University-Small Business Technology Consortium, and the Small Business Innovation Research (SBIR) grant program in North Dakota.

LORD PUBLISHING, INC., 1988

Preface

*"Never tell people how to do things.
Tell them what to do and they will
surprise you with their ingenuity."*
General George S. Patton, Jr.

This quote is fitting for today's entrepreneurial spirit and reflects the spirit of this publication. America is experiencing a boom in new business start-ups. Entrepreneurs are the heros. They develop new products, they encourage innovation, they create new jobs. Unfortunately, many of them fail because they don't know what they are getting into to begin with. This knowledge gap has given rise to "entrepreneurial consultants" and "new business experts." There are probably as many "professional advisors" out there as there are new business startups. Because each new business start-up is different, a lot of this advice is confusing and even conflicting.

This Business Planning Guide is a series of exercises. It tells you *what* to do (or be thinking about), not *how* to do it. Starting a business requires perseverance. You must take initiative and utilize whatever resources are available to you. We don't have all the answers and there is no way we can tell you where to go to find them without making this publication so voluminous, it would be unreadable. The guide may be imposing for some, as is, but it is so by necessity. Writing a business plan can be a time consuming and tedious task. It can also be very enlightening and rewarding. No matter what your objective may be with a start-up venture, you stand a much better chance of profiting from it with a well thought out business plan.

This guide was written to help you identify basic issues, address the details, and write a comprehensive business plan. First and foremost, it is a guide that recognizes that effective business plans must be tailored to unique circumstances. There are many "how to" publications and seminars being promoted about business planning that do not truly embrace this simple fact in their material. They may be good for motivating people, but usually they neglect the details involved in starting or expanding a venture, along with the features that make it unique. Each venture has its own problems and opportunities, and each must address distinct issues that are separate from other kinds of start-ups.

LORD PUBLISHING, INC., 1988

What To Do

In keeping with General Patton's advice, there are three other things you should do before you prepare your business plan.

First, you can save considerable time and produce a better business plan if you do a "venture feasibility analysis" before working on this guide. Our companion piece, *Venture Feasibility Planning Guide*, describes this process.

Second, the financials produced for a good business plan are often the most difficult and time)consuming aspect of business planning for most entrepreneurs. You cannot delegate this part of "your" plan to others. You need to know the numbers. The best treatment of this topic is *Entrepreneurial Finance: Taking Control of Your Financial Decision Making*. This short book will introduce you to the key issues and questions about financing your venture.

Third, the actual development of your financials and their subsequent revision (as you develop your enterprise and revise your business plan) is handled best by the software, *Ronstadt's FINANCIALS*. This standalone program runs on IBM PCs and compatibles. It contains great finance, accounting, and entrepreneurial expertise, requires minimal training, and generates linked or integrated financial projections, including revenue statements, income statements, balance sheets, cash flow statements, key measures, and breakeven statements. If you are not computer inclined, we've included guidelines in this planning guide for you to produce manual calculations. However, you should recognize this approach has definite limitations in answering key questions about your likely cash requirements, about the timing of these cash needs, and about alternative financial strategies.

Introduction

Introduction

How High Can You Jump?

You need to feel comfortable with why you must go through the exercise of writing a business plan. If you don't understand the reasons and benefits it will bring, in all likelihood you will do a less than an adequate job. You will defeat your purpose before you ever get started. To be sure, writing a business plan is one of those hoops you must jump through. The players (investors, customers, suppliers, etc.) are simply not going to let you play until you are good enough to be on the team. Besides, if you can't put your plan on paper, then you haven't really thought it out. You may think this is an exercise in futility, especially since times and events change, and your company will certainly change with them. And that is exactly why you need to have a business plan.

Your plan must reflect your ultimate goal. Be honest up front. What will be the extent of your involvement? Do you want to own and/or manage this startup? If so, be prepared to show why you are capable and how you will compensate in the areas that you have no expertise. Perhaps your real aim is to sell your idea or license your product to an existing company in exchange for royalties. Your plan must be written according to what *YOU* want. You must then tailor it to a specific use.

The Uses of a Business Plan

Your plan can accomplish many things for you and your proposed venture, but it is not prudent to try to make it be all things to all people. One plan will simply not suffice for all possible uses. Indeed, most seasoned entrepreneurs will write (or revise) a business plan at each stage of the company's development. The most successful of these will then write several plans, each adapted for specific players.

Sounds like a pain, doesn't it? Actually, it is not that difficult or time consuming. Once you have done your homework and decided to go ahead, it doesn't take much more effort to expand and/or adapt a business plan. The basic format of a plan is essentially the same for all uses. The trick is to beef up the sections that are of most interest to your target audience: investors, the management team, suppliers, customers, etc.

LORD PUBLISHING, INC., 1988

A Development Tool

A plan of this nature is written for yourself, your partner(s) if you have any, and any other principals concerned with the startup. You will want to concentrate on the section dealing with overall schedule and milestones (Module 12). This plan functions as a detailed "to do" list. It helps you set realistic deadlines and delegate assignments. It keeps you on track in the early stages.

At this point, the other sections of your plan are sketchy, just some initial thoughts on how you think (or would like) the whole venture to come together. It serves as a blueprint for filling in the details in the other sections and substantiating "how" and "why" your idea will be successful. If your objective is to develop your idea along just far enough to prove it feasible, then sell it and go on to something else, then tailor your plan to that objective.

A Management and Planning Guide

If you're in for the long haul, this is the plan you want to develop. This use is at the heart of all good plans. Since it is the most comprehensive, most of the other uses of a business plan are adapted from this one.

This type of plan becomes an operating bible for the *management* of your company. Since you can't predict the future, the best you can do is monitor and measure actual performance against expected performance. When events deviate from your plan, you can quickly take corrective action.

This use forces you to identify opportunities and threats, strengths and weaknesses. It will prompt you and your associates to agree upon goals, strategies, and objectives in a systematic and realistic manner. You will want to concentrate on the sections dealing with Operations, Management and Ownership, Administration, Organization and Personnel (Modules 9, 10, and 11).

A Mission Statement

No matter what stage of development your idea may be in, you are going to have to let certain key people know what you are all about. This type of plan is used to team up with suppliers, inform consultants and other professionals that may be needed (lawyers, accountants, etc.), and to pre-commit customers. You will not always be granted a forum to explain in person what they need to know to act on your idea. You should always be prepared to give them a plan to review — one that is tailored to their interest or expertise.

An overview of each section may be appropriate, but you may not want to share detailed or confidential information with certain parties. For suppliers, it may be appropriate to beef up the section on the Product and the Technological or Manufacturing Operations. It may be that if suppliers knew these things, they could pose a competitive threat. Use your judgment, giving each player a plan that goes into detail in sections that are applicable to them, while giving only a brief sketch of the other sections.

A Sales Document   The vast majority of business plans are written exclusively for this use. Most end up as nothing more than shallow sales material. Sophisticated investors recognize these right away and pitch them in the circular file. No one can deny that a good business plan is one that raises money as long as all sections are well researched and documented and the financial projections and assumptions can be substantiated.

If you're going to romance money, you have to have appeal. The problem is, what excites one person doesn't necessarily excite another. Again, you will have to tailor this kind of plan to the type of financing you are seeking (or think you stand the best chance of getting). It is not unusual for some entrepreneurs to cover all the bases by writing several plans, each designed to address the interests and concerns of the different financial groups.

Bankers, for instance, are usually more conservative than venture capitalist and private investors. They will be primarily interested in the company's fixed assets (building, equipment, etc.) and the collateral you can offer. They often don't care how innovative your idea is, what industry you are in, or how many trillions of dollars you are going to make. They just want to know if their loan can be paid back at the going interest rate.

Venture capitalists (and other sophisticated independent investment groups, by any other name) are more willing to roll the dice. They may want a chunk of your company and its profits for their risk. They like innovative products and services that address a growth or "glamor" industry. They want to earn at least a 45 percent compounded annual Return on Investment (ROI one of those catchy phrases people like to see in a business plan). **In other words, they want to get back six times their money in 3-5 years.** The sections to beef up for this use are, in order of importance: the Executive Summary, the Financial Data and Projections (particularly a current balance sheet and terms of the deal); the Management Team, and the Product or Service.

Private investors are the most common financiers of startups. They are usually family, friends, and other well wishers who want you out of their hair, but have a sincere desire to see you succeed. These people can't be taken for granted. Many of today's most successful companies were started in garages just this way. They deserve to see a plan, especially if you want them to take you seriously. After all, business is business.

Limited partnerships and other types of deals can also be structured through more sophisticated private investors. If you are targeting local investors to fund your startup, they look for who else is in the deal. They like to see a big name they know (or have heard of) and respect. You will want to beef up the section on Management, particularly the Board of Directors.

Very simply, a plan tells the reader where you have been, where you are now, and where you hope to go. Don't worry about raising money at this point. Money will be attracted to a good business idea which can be feasibly implemented. There are plenty of avenues open. Your first objective is to write a good plan that can be tailored to a specific use. Just don't lose sight of the fact you are writing the plan as much for yourself as anyone else.

Who Should Write the Plan?

You should write the business plan.

So, you may not be a literary genius. That's not the point. It is the process, not the writing, that counts. If someone else writes the plan, then it is *their* plan, not *yours*. The people interested in this startup want to see that you know and understand the functional areas of a company. They want to be sure you have the big picture and will pay attention to the details as well. If you cannot write it for lack of time or circumstance, you should maintain as much control and direction in the writing as possible.

"...remember, people buy people. Most products and services cannot be patented. Contrary to popular belief, you can build a better mousetrap but the world *will not* beat a path to your door. A plan is only as good as the people who implement it. Investors put more stock in the management than they do the product. That is why there is generally more money chasing well developed ideas than there are ideas chasing money..." These statements are all cliches often heard in the venture capital world. They are reinforced here because they are all true.

Investors know that if your business plan is not done right, you probably will never do anything of substance beyond it. This guide gives you what you need to demonstrate the credibility and competence of a workable plan. The confidence and commitment to get through it can only come from you. In this sense, the guide serves as architect and engineer. It will help you build a well designed plan that is structurally sound. You're the builder. What you put into it — the thought, research, facts and figures, and other information — are the bricks and mortar.

Authenticity and Style

You may have noticed that this guide takes an unusually informal and personal approach. It is unique because it doesn't look or talk like a textbook. Its purpose is to communicate with you, not impress you with complicated theories and formulas.

LORD PUBLISHING, INC., 1988

Your business plan is uniquely yours. Use your own style. It should be a personal expression (an art form) as much as a professional document (scientifically and structurally sound). Feel free to express yourself in the first person (we, I, ours). In your first draft do not be overly concerned with spelling, punctuation and grammar. Let it flow naturally from your heart and mind, utilizing your research notes and experience. Someone who writes well can help you put the finishing touches on it later. For an excellent guide on writing, check out *Elements of Style,* Strunk and White. This paperback should be available through your local library.

You will want your work to transmit enthusiasm, but try to avoid using flowery language and superlatives. Phrases like, "Fantastic sales" and "Tremendous profits" send up red flags and will lessen the impact of truly significant messages. There are certain words and phrases that investors and other professionals do look for (like ROI). These are noted in each section in bold print and a glossary is included to help you understand the lingo. Incorporate them into your text in your own way. Above all, use clear layman's language. Remember, some of the people who will be reading your plan will know nothing about your product, the technological or manufacturing process involved, or even the industry it addresses.

Writing One That Works

Writing a business plan is tough work. A typical timeframe for writing a plan would exceed 300 hours over one to six months, depending on how much time can be devoted to the research and writing. The plan must be comprehensive, but concise. Only in exceptional cases should they exceed fifty pages (typewritten/double spaced), and twenty-five pages would be a good target. A too sketchy plan will be viewed as evidence the entrepreneur has not done his or her homework — sure grounds for rejection. If it is too long and brought in on a wheelbarrow, it won't be read, which is the same as rejection. You have to write a plan that people will read and give them confidence in you and your idea.

The Executive Summary

The most important section of your business plan is the executive summary. After months of work, if you haven't sold the business opportunity in the first five minutes of reading, you have lost your reader. If not excited on the first two pages, the reader certainly won't hunt through the chapters for what makes your venture truly unique and worthy of support. The executive summary should highlight the most significant points of your business plan and entice the reader to read on. In six paragraphs, the following needs to be described:

1. your product and why it is unique and profitable,

2. what business you are in and the milestones reached with financial results,

3. what is the market for your product, what size it will be, and your share of the market,

4. the management team and their expertise,

5. what are the financial terms and profit potential, and

6. what your unique strengths and advantages are that will contribute to the success of this venture.

It is best to write the executive summary after you have written the rest of the business plan, because that exercise will also help you sort out the important information.

Financial Information

The next most important portion of the business plan is your financial projections — after all you are in business for profits. The financial section should clearly indicate the amount of funds needed and what those funds would be used for. This section is highly scrutinized by the people with money. If the company is already in operation, you will need to provide a profit and loss statement and a balance sheet. An existing or startup company needs to provide projections for these statements for a three to five year period. These statements should indicate the upside, downside, and expected financial results.

It is also to your advantage to provide a breakeven analysis. The five-year requirements may seem impossible to meet with any accuracy and often is. One solution is to generate three scenarios for the five-year period. Use conservative projections based on a weak market performance, aggressive projections based on robust demand, and the most likely results of your efforts. It is also recommended that you explain key assumptions and show how the numbers were derived. Prepare to justify your figures.

The Management Team

After the reader has summed up the unique business opportunity and the financial projections, the final determination is whether the entrepreneur can really do the job. The credibility of the business plan will be under siege, and if it survives the analysis, the focus will be on the entrepreneur and if they can meet company objectives and make money. The management section of the business plan must outline experience, expertise, and past accomplishments, and the tone of the business plan must be honest and evoke trust. The entrepreneur has to identify the weaknesses and negatives and address them. The reader wants to reduce his risk, and he wants to know if you are doing that.

If the reader is still with you, they will finish reading the business plan with a critical eye. If you have managed, however, to romance your reader, they may be looking for the reasons why they should support your business opportunity. If interested, they are selling themselves and justifying their decision. Write the rest of the chapters well, and give them the reasons why they should be involved.

What To Avoid

Most bankers, investors, venture capitalists, and consultants have too much to do in too little time, so entrepreneurs need to avoid the turnoffs often associated with business plans. We have already talked about being too long or too short. The business plan needs to be "crisp," indicating clearly and concisely what this venture is all about. Readers expect a professional business plan, neatly typed with no spelling errors, but a too polished business plan with a fancy cover raises eyebrows and red flags. The emphasis should be on substance, not on form and style. Other turnoffs include a poor marketing plan, failing to identify details about competitors, not identifying key employees, weaknesses in the management team, massive advertising budgets, high salaries, and unrealistic sales forecasts.

Remember, you want to push the hot button of your reader, not raise flags and eyebrows. Do your homework, evaluate it critically, and check it again. Whether the reader is you, your partners, your Uncle Harry, the banker, or a venture capitalist, your business plan is written for a good purpose.

In Summary

A business plan is a necessary exercise, often required by investors, suppliers, and customers. Most importantly, it is a vital planning tool for the entrepreneur.

■ A business plan must reflect the entrepreneur's ultimate goal for the venture.

■ A business plan may be tailored for several uses:

    – as a development tool for the founders

    – as a planning and evaluation guide for the managers and other

■ Expect to spend a minimum of 300 hours developing the business plan. Planning is a vital component to properly and strategically position a new venture. It is your road map to business success.

■ By the way, some people will tell you that researching and writing a business plan that results in the successful startup of a company is equivalent to an MBA degree any day. While this statement is certainly debatable, no one can argue that the experience is an educational one. An exciting one at that. Good luck and many happy revenues!

The Modular Approach

LORD
PUBLISHING

The Modular Approach

A Word on Format

This guide is written in modular format, where each module represents a "chapter" or "section" of a good business plan. Each module is designed to stand alone. It assumes that people collect, organize, and absorb information in blocks, rather than in large doses. While keeping the "big picture" in perspective, this guide attempts to make writing the business plan a series of mini lessons. Work one module at a time. There is no reason to frustrate yourself with too much material or information at once.

Some modules may not apply to you. If yours is a service business, the module on product manufacturing will be of little interest. Pick and choose what you need. Most of the modules are part of a well designed business plan which must be addressed by all startup companies in any industry. Depending upon the scope of the venture, it may be appropriate to combine and condense several modules into one section.

Each module breaks down the essential components of a business plan. They are presented in logical sequence, in workbook fashion. Each module will tell you:

Suggested Length of the Section

This is purely a judgment call. Use as much space as you need, but be concise and to the point. Business plans less than ten pages long have been known to raise millions, but rarely. Again, the length will be largely determined by the intended use of the plan. Avoid the "wheel barrel" approach. These plans are so long, you need two people to lift them. Too much information is as damaging as too little information. It only confuses and overwhelms the reader. All totalled, your plan should not exceed 50 pages (not including appendices), typewritten, double spaced.

Objective of the Module

This is why the entire module is written.

LORD PUBLISHING, INC., 1988

Questions Which Must be Answered

This part of each module is the most important aspect of this guide. The questions are thought provokers. They are not all inclusive. They *do not* cover *every* issue you might be concerned with, but they cover at least the basics and will lead you to uncover and address other issues. The questions not only help you discover issues you should include in your business plan, they also prepare you for the verbal firing line when you go before prospective investors. These are the questions that *will* be asked of you — you can count on it! No one expects you to have all the answers. They *do* expect you to know most of the questions, and want to know how you are thinking about attacking these issues. (Some of the same issues are covered in two or more modules. Therefore, you will find some redundancy. In order to be thorough and allow each module to stand alone, this couldn't be avoided.)

Subheadings to Include

This simply highlights the most important aspects of each module of your business plan. Subheadings help make your plan more readable. The subheadings we recommend are standard issues of each topic. They are only suggestions. Include whatever subheadings you think appropriate for your situation.

Description of What to Accomplish Under Each Subheading

This is *how* each issue will be addressed. It is a guide to refer to as you outline and write each module. Again, it is not all inclusive. Your gut feelings and unique style will be your best guide as you develop and write each module.

A List of Common Mistakes to Avoid

This will help you ensure the integrity of each module of your plan. Most plans fail because of the same pitfalls and weaknesses. These lists try to identify most of them for you. You may want to glance over them *before* you write each module. After you write each module, study this list closely and recheck your work. It is also wise to have an objective friend or advisor look over the list and then read what you have written. They will be more apt to pick up on common mistakes.

The order of sequence in which each module appears was carefully chosen. Research indicates this is the preferred order of review among investors, bankers, and other professionals. It is not carved in stone. The order of sequence for the contents of your plan is entirely up to you. A reader who has a particular interest in a certain module can find it in the table of contents and go right to it.

There is one trap to avoid as you begin. **The order of sequence in which your plan's contents will appear is not necessarily the order in which you will research and write each module.** For example, the Executive Summary appears first, but is usually the last module to be written. The first thing you need is market information. Second, can your idea be put into a *profitable* plan of action? Therefore, the market research and financial projections are usually most important. All other modules are developed from these.

Suggestions on How to Proceed

1. Flip through this entire guide to acquaint yourself with the modules. Decide if you should combine one or more modules into one section (see Module 2 — Table of Contents)

2. Decide where you would like (or should) begin. Complete one module at a time. It is suggested that you start with Module 3 or 6.

3. Make sure you understand the objective of each module. Keep the objective foremost in your mind as you write that module of your plan.

4. Read through each module carefully, noting areas where you will have to do some additional research before you area able to answer the questions. If a question does not apply to your situation you should cross it out. This will help you keep a positive attitude by making your task appear less tedious.

5. Pick up your pencil and go to work! You should not expect to complete each module on your first attempt, but do as much as you can the first time through.

6. Continue to work on the questions not yet answered until you have completed the module. Do not feel constrained by the space allowed for each question. If you need additional space either write in the margins or on a separate sheet of paper.

7. Decide on the subheadings you want to include in each module. Using the "description of what to accomplish" as a guide, outline each subheading according to your research and experience as reflected by your answers to the questions.

8. Write each module of the business plan in your own style according to the outlines provided.

9. Critique your work for each module using the list of "Common Mistakes to Avoid."

10. Have your plan proofread by a person well versed in English grammar. Have it reviewed by your accountant and other professional advisors. Finally, have it bound in an attractive binder (see "Packaging Your Business Plan." under the "Finishing Touches" section).

Module 1 — The Executive Summary

Suggested Length   1–3 pages

Objective   To get the reader to keep on reading; to highlight the most significant points of each module.

Pertinent Questions

1. What type of venture is this? (Check and describe)

    ☐ merchandising

    ☐ manufacturing/processing

    ☐ distribution

    ☐ service

    ☐ other _____

    _____

    _____

    _____

2. What products/services will it offer?

    _____

    _____

    _____

    Why are they unique?

    _____

    _____

    _____

    Do they solve a significant problem?

    _____

    _____

    _____

    Do they address a major opportunity?

    _____

    _____

    _____

3. What is the business status? (Check and describe)

    ☐ startup

    ☐ takeover

    ☐ expansion

    ☐ other _____

    _____

    _____

    _____

    _____

4. What stage is this venture in? (Check and describe)

    ☐ research and development

    ☐ prototype

    ☐ operational

    _____

    _____

    _____

5. How long has the business been operating? (or been in development)

    _____ months   _____ years

6. What will be the form of organization? (Check and describe)

    ☐ proprietorship

    ☐ partnership (type)

    ☐ corporation (type)

    _____

    _____

    _____

    _____

7. Where will the business be located?

    _____

    _____

    _____

    What is advantageous about this location?

    _____

    _____

    _____

8. Who and what is the target market?

9. What percent of the available market will you obtain?

What is your plan and strategy for entering the market?

10. Who is the competition?

What are their strengths and weaknesses?

What is their market share?

11. Who is going to manage the business?

_____

_____

_____

_____

What qualifications are needed to manage this business?

_____

_____

_____

_____

What is the experience, education, and background of the principals?

_____

_____

_____

_____

12. What are the timeframes for accomplishing the milestones and goals?

_____

_____

_____

_____

13. How much money is needed to make this venture successful?

_____

_____

_____

How much money is needed for product improvement?

_____

_____

How much money is needed for marketing?

_____

_____

_____

How much money is needed for operations?

_____

_____

_____

14. What kind of financing are you looking for? (Check and describe)
    ☐ debt
    ☐ equity

    _____

    _____

    _____

    _____

15. What are you offering in return? (Check and describe.)
    ☐ ownership (how much?)
    ☐ share of profits (projected earnings over 3–5 years)
    ☐ other _____

    _____

    _____

    _____

16. What is the payback period?

    _____

    _____

    _____

17. How much money has been invested to date?

    _____

    _____

    _____

18. What is your interest (financial and otherwise) and long-term objective?

    _____

    _____

    _____

    _____

LORD PUBLISHING, INC., 1988

19. What are the strengths of the business? (What will make it successful)? (Check and describe.)

    ☐ management

    ☐ skilled/experienced personnel

    ☐ unique product/service

    ☐ constant source of supply

    ☐ low production/overhead

    ☐ high margin

    ☐ good service

    ☐ emphasis on quality

    _____

    _____

    _____

    _____

    _____

20. What are the limitations on the business? (Check and describe)

    ☐ capital

    ☐ management resources

    ☐ personnel

    ☐ other _____

    _____

    _____

    _____

    _____

    _____

21. What are the venture's long range growth and expansion objectives?

    _____

    _____

    _____

    _____

    _____

Subheadings to Include

The Executive Summary is one complete Module. A Fact Summary Sheet at the back of the section is recommended.

What to Accomplish

The entire summary should be clear and to the point. Use short, choppy phrases. The language should be simple and demonstrate clarity of management objectives. Above all, the summary should *show opportunity!*

The following is a suggested sequence of presentation:

Concept

The opening statement should grab attention. State something about being the first to introduce this product or the customer demands being generated from your initial market research. Describe the nature of the business; i.e., type, location, business form, length, and state of operation. Describe current milestones reached and their financial results; i.e., reaching X amount in sales, evaluation and testing completed, prototype built. State what industry your product addresses.

Product/Service

Describe your product. Discuss specialization, significant, or unique features. Discuss where you are, or would like to be located. State why this location will be advantageous. If the product is to be sold or distributed through other outlets, discuss how this will be done and their locations. Describe any precommitted sales or contractual relationships you have with manufacturers and/or distributors for your product.

Market

Describe the market for your product, your current or projected share, and overall potential. Discuss the competition and what advantages you have over them. Discuss your plans for introducing your product and your strategy for gaining market acceptance and loyalty. Mention any letters of intent you have with prospective customers.

Manufacturing/Operations

Discuss the processes involved in producing your product and getting it into the marketplace. Highlight areas of specialization and technology that you may have pioneered in the production of the product. If you plan to subcontract or license Manufacturing/Operations, describe the arrangement and why it is advantageous.

Management

Discuss the people involved in the venture, their management expertise and experience. Highlight their distinctive competence. Discuss support personnel that will be needed as the company grows. Show that the people involved are qualified and committed.

Funding Request and Times of Investment

State how much money has been invested to date in the venture. State the additional funds needed and their use. Discuss what you are offering in return for the money. Include the payback period and potential return on investment. State what the earning projections are for the next 3–5 years. State any tax benefits that will result from investment.

Milestones and Timeframes

State what must be done and expected completion date to move venture along. Describe the phases and timeframes with which the business will be concerned. Summarize the unique advantages and strengths that will contribute to the success of the venture.

Common Mistakes to Avoid

- Too wordy; not to the point
- Too long; trying to be all inclusive
- Does not identify a special or unique opportunity
- Does not clearly demonstrate what the venture is all about
- Does not identify what management hopes to accomplish and how they plan to go about it
- Terms of the deal are not clear
- Failure to insure all the proper legal steps have been taken (see Fact Sheet)

The Fact Sheet stands alone and appears at the back of the Executive Summary Module as a separate page. It enables the reader to scan the vital information that makes up the company. Fill in the following fact sheet **and** have it typed on a separate page.

FACT SHEET

Name of Company:

Location: (address, city, county, state, zip, phone)

Zoning Classification: (obtain from city ordinance)

Type of Business and Industry: (example — manufacturing, agriculture)

Business Form: (proprietorship, partnership [type], corporation [type])

Product or Service Line: (example — electronics, household)

Patent, Trademark or Service Mark: (type, number, date issued)

Length of time in business (or in development)

Number of Founders/partners/employees:

Current and/or projected share of market: (example — 10% of GF market 1985, 20% 1986)

Invested to Date: (estimate equipment, supplies, time)

Net Worth:

Additional Financing Needed: (estimate total dollar amount)

Minimum Investment: (dollar amount for stock, partnership unit, etc.)

Terms and Payback Period: (example — equity position, limited partnership shares, 3-year buyback, 40% ROI)

Total Valuation: (after placement):

Legal Counsel:

Financial Counsel:

Management Counsel:

Description of any related party transactions, contracts, or relationships which the company may be involved in.

Module 2 — The Table of Contents

Suggested Length	1–2 pages
Objective	To allow the reader to quickly access particular sections of interest.
Pertinent Questions	1. What are the pertinent sections (topics) that you should include in your plan? What are the appropriate subheadings of each? 2. In what order will you present the contents? 3. What pictures, graphs, legal documents, etc. should you include as supporting material? 4. Given the nature of the business and purpose for which you are writing the plan, how long (number of pages) will this plan be?
Subheadings to Include	The following is a list of topics or issues you might include. Depending on the importance of each issue to your startup, any one can stand alone as a separate section or be combined with another issue. Also listed are possible subheadings that may be organized under each main topic.

The Company
    Background
    Current Status
    Future Plans

The Industry
    Chief Characteristics
    The Participants
    Analyst Summaries
    Trends

Product and Related Services
    Product/Service Description
    Facilities Description
    Proprietary Features
    Future Development Plans
    Product Liability

Technology: Research and Development
        Concept Development
        Research, Testing and Evaluation
        Milestones and Breakthroughs
        Current Status and Continuing R&D

Market Analysis
        Target Market and Characteristics
        Analyst Summaries
        Market Share, Trends, and Growth Potential
        Sales, Distribution, and Profits by Product/Service

Competitive Analysis
        Competitors Profile
        Product/Services Comparison
        Market Niche and Share
        Comparison of Strengths and Weaknesses

Marketing Strategy
        Penetration Goals
        Pricing and Packaging
        Sales and Distribution
        Service and Warranty Policies
        Advertising, Public Relations, and Promotions

Manufacturing Process and Operations
        Location
        Facilities and Equipment
        Manufacturing Process and Operations
        Labor Considerations
        Environmental and Economic Impact

Management and Ownership
        Key People and Experience
        Board of Directors
        Ownership Distribution and Incentives
        Professional Support Services

Administration, Organization, and Personnel
        Administrative Procedures and Controls
        Staffing and Training
        Organizational Chart
        Management Control Systems

Milestones, Schedule, and Strategic Planning
        Major Milestones (What/Why)
        Schedule (When/Who)
        Strategic Planning (How/Where)

LORD PUBLISHING, INC., 1988

Critical Risks and Problems
    Summary of Major Problems Overcome
    Inevitable Risks and Problems
    Potential Risks and Problems
    Worst Case Scenarios

Financial Data and Projections
    Funding Request/Terms of Investment
    Current Financial Statements
    Financial Projections
    Assumptions

Appendices

The following is a condensed version of the Table of Contents utilizing all the modules.

Executive Summary

  I. Business Summary
    A. The Company and the Industry
    B. Management and Ownership
    C. Administration, Organization, and Personnel

  II. The Product and Services
    A. The Technology: Research and Development
    B. Manufacturing and Operations

  III. The Market
    A. Market Analysis
    B. Competitive Analysis
    C. Marketing Strategy

  IV. Schedule and Risks

  V. Financial Data

  VI. Appendices

What to Accomplish

All major sections should be listed in bold print in the order in which they appear in the plan. Designate each major section with a Roman Numeral along the lefthand margin. All major sections and subheadings should have a corresponding page number listed along the righthand margin. Example:

I. The Company 1

    Background 2
    Current Status 2
    Future Plans 3

II. The Industry 4

    Chief Characteristics 5
    The Participants 5
    Analysts Summaries................................... 5
    Trend 6

LORD PUBLISHING, INC., 1988

Common Mistakes to Avoid

- Prominent sections of interest are not discernible
- Page numbers are not clearly marked for each section
- Sequence of topic presentation follows a confusing or illogical pattern
- Listing certain subheadings under unrelated major sections

LORD PUBLISHING, INC., 1988

Module 3 — The Company and the Industry

Suggested Length   1–3 pages

Objective   To describe the startup and background of your company. To provide a brief sketch of your industry and how your venture addresses it.

Note: The first part of this Module is primarily for ventures that have some operating history. If your company has a significant history, you may want to have this section stand alone as its own chapter.

Pertinent Questions   1. When and where was the company started?

_____

_____

_____

Date and state of incorporation or partnership?

_____

_____

_____

2. What is the form of organization?

_____

_____

_____

Will this be changing? when?

_____

_____

_____

3. Where is the business located?

_____

_____

_____

Will you, or have you changed locations?

_____

Why?

_____

_____

_____

4. How long have you been in business?

_____

_____

_____

5. Did you obtain a patent or trademark for the company's name and/or logo?

_____

Do you have one pending?

_____

6. Why did you go into business?

_____

_____

_____

7. How was this business venture developed?

_____

_____

_____

How long did it take?

_____

What problems were encountered?

_____

_____

_____

How were they overcome?

_____

_____

_____

_____

What were the key milestones?

_____

_____

_____

How and when were they accomplished?

_____

_____

_____

_____

8. Who are the founders and other key people involved?

_____

_____

_____

_____

What do they bring to the business?

_____

_____

_____

_____

_____

9. How did you identify your market?

_____

_____

_____

_____

_____

What success have you had in penetrating it?

_____

_____

_____

_____

10. How have you dealt with the competition?

_____

_____

_____

_____

11. What are your overall strengths and weaknesses?

_____

_____

_____

_____

12. How much money have you invested?

_____

_____

_____

What has been your source of funding?

_____

_____

_____

How has the money been used?

_____

_____

_____

Is the investment secured? How?

_____

_____

13. What are you future goals and strategy for achieving them?

_____

_____

_____

_____

_____

14. How is your company affected by major economic, social, technological, environmental or regulatory trends?

_____

_____

_____

_____

_____

_____

15. What is your sales and service record?

_____

_____

_____

_____

16. What industry are you in?

_____

_____

17. What is the current state of the industry?

_____

_____

_____

How big is it?

_____

Total sales? profits? margins?

_____

_____

18. Who are the major industry participants (competitors, suppliers, major customers, distributors, etc.)?

_____

_____

_____

_____

What is their performance? market share?

_____

_____

_____

_____

What advantages do you have over them?

_____

_____

_____

_____

How will you capture markets others are competing for?

_____

_____

_____

19. What are the industry's chief characteristics?

_____

_____

_____

_____

Where is it expected to be in 5 years? 10 years?

_____

_____

_____

_____

Will your share increase or decrease with these changes?

_____

_____

_____

Who else may get into the industry?

_____

_____

_____

Subheadings to Include

The Company
    Background
    Current Status
    Future Plans

The Industry
    Chief Characteristics
    The Participants
    Analyst Summaries
    Trends

What to Accomplish

Make the reader a part of your dreams. Describe how your work and decisions got the company where it is. Show how past performance will pave the way to future success. Demonstrate how you will become an important addition to the industry, that you understand the industry, and where it is headed.

The following is a suggested sequence of presentation:

THE COMPANY

Background

Describe the startup and history of your company from the time of inception. State where and when it was organized. State what form of business it is and where it is located. Discuss significant milestones, such as obtaining a patent, building a prototype, or signing a major contract. Discuss the people involved and the roles they have played. Mention any trademarks on the company's name or logo.

Current Status

Discuss where you are now. Talk about the reputation you have built, your strengths and what limitations are being experienced. Describe how your product is performing in the marketplace. State the amount of money that has been invested to date, by whom, and how it has been used. Give an overview of your sales and services record, if any. Discuss the kind and amount of funding the business needs to begin operations or improve operations.

Future Plans

Discuss your goals for the next 3–5 years. Describe how you plan to achieve them and what resources will be needed. Allude to improvements and expansion of your existing product line, as well as your hopes for increasing your market share and sales.

THE INDUSTRY

Chief Characteristics

Describe the industry your company is in. Discuss the industry's profile, including: size, geographical dispersion, market, history summation, current status, and its total sales and profits for each of the last three years.

The Participants

Discuss the competition and other players (suppliers, wholesalers, distributors, etc.) within your industry. Summarize each participant along a spectrum of weakest to strongest. Briefly discuss their product/service lines and market niche. Discuss more thoroughly the participants with whom you will have direct involvement or competition.

Analyst Summaries

Provide a series of quotes and statements that summarize significant facts, figures, and trends about the industry from various reputable sources. Make sure you properly credit the source and provide the date of publication. Use quotes and statements from diverse sources; i.e., industry magazines and newspaper articles. Quotes from personal interviews can also have a powerful impact. These statements should clarify where the industry is headed and the various markets to be served within the industry.

Industry Trends

Discuss where you industry is headed. State whether it is declining, improving, or holding steady and what opportunities there may be. Discuss where it might be in 5–10 years and your relative position within it. Discuss the future of the industry in terms of market need and/or acceptance and profit potential. Describe significant events or changes within the industry that will affect your business positively or negatively.

Common Mistakes to Avoid

- Too much detail and personal opinion about the company, not enough on significant milestones and potential

- Not demonstrating a well-rounded knowledge of major industry players and their potential influence on the company.

- Appears to by a "fly-by-night" operation

- Lack of direction and commitment evident

- Poor or inadequate knowledge of the industry and trends

Module 4 — Product and Related Services

Suggested Length   1–3 pages

Objective   To describe the product and related services, special features, benefits, and future development plans.

Pertinent Questions

1. What is the purpose of the product/services?

   _____

   _____

   _____

   Do they solve a problem or address an opportunity?

   _____

   _____

   _____

   Are they luxury items or need items?

   _____

   _____

   _____

2. How does the product achieve this purpose?

   _____

   _____

   _____

3. What are its unique features? (cost, design, quality, capabilities, etc.)

   _____

   _____

   _____

   _____

4. What is its technological life?

   _____

   _____

LORD PUBLISHING, INC., 1988

How does it compare with state of the art?

_____

_____

What is its susceptibility to obsolescence?

_____

_____

To change in style or fashion?

_____

_____

5. What stage of development is the product in? (Check and describe)
   ☐ idea
   ☐ model
   ☐ working prototype
   ☐ small production runs
   ☐ full manufacturing/production (at what level?)
   ☐ engineering prototype
   ☐ production prototype

_____

_____

_____

_____

6. How will the product be produced?

_____

_____

_____

Is it capital intensive?

_____

_____

Is it labor intensive?

_____

_____

Is it material intensive?

_____

_____

7. Will all or some of production be subcontracted?

_____

_____

_____

8. Is this an end-use item or a component of another product?

_____

_____

Does your company's survival depend on someone else?

_____

_____

_____

9. Can your product be protected by patent, copyright, trademark or servicemark? What protection will be provided?

_____

_____

10. Do you interface with important, noncompetitive equipment whose manufacturer might be reluctant to support your product due to warranty, liability or image considerations?

_____

_____

_____

11. What new products (spinoffs) do you plan to develop to meet changing market needs, in this industry or others?

_____

_____

_____

12. What are the regulatory or approval requirements from government agencies, or other industry participants?

_____

_____

_____

_____

13. Is the product dependent on any natural, industry or market life cycles? What cycle? (Check and describe)

    ☐ introduction

    ☐ growth

    ☐ maturity

    _____

    _____

    _____

    _____

14. What are the liabilities this product may pose?

    _____

    _____

    _____

    What are the insurance requirements?

    _____

    _____

15. What kind of engineering studies, testing and evaluation has the product undergone?

    _____

    _____

    _____

16. If more than one product is involved, how will the manufacture and/or promotion of one affect the other?

    _____

    _____

    _____

17. How does this product compare to similar products of competitors?

    _____

    _____

    _____

    _____

18. What are any special manufacturing or technological considerations?

_____

_____

_____

What are the maintenance/updating requirements?

_____

_____

_____

19. If equipment is involved, what is its reliability factor?

_____

_____

What is it's downtime?

_____

20. What are the related services you will provide?

_____

_____

_____

How will they enhance and increase the profitability of the venture?

_____

_____

_____

Subheadings to Include	Description of Product/Service Description of the Facilities Proprietary Features Future Development Plans Product Liability
What to Accomplish	In layman's language, explain your product and services, what they do (that's special or different), and who they serve. Briefly highlight future plans for improvements or for introducing new products/services.

The following is a suggested sequence of presentation:

Product/Service Description

Describe exactly what your product/service is and for what it was designed. Discuss how it works, special features, capabilities, and resulting benefits (economic, social, environmental, leisure, etc.). If more than one service or product line is involved, discuss each one and how they function together and/or affect each other. State what stage of development the product/service is in.

Facilities Description

If the facilities are a focus and part of the product or service (such as a hotel would be), describe them in this section. If the facilities are an adjunct, rather than interrelated with the product or service (such as a machine manufacturing and assembly plant), it would be best to describe them along with the operations description in Module 9.

Describe the facilities and why they are unique or better; i.e., none other like it, more attractive, better proximity to customer base, offers more, etc. Discuss location and why it is advantageous. State what percentage of the facilities are used for revenue producing services, operations, storage, etc.

Proprietary Features

Discuss any patents, copyrights, trademarks, servicemarks, or other legally binding agreements that protect your product or service. State if a patent is pending. Overall, discuss how you intend to protect the integrity, confidentiality and competitive nature of your product and services. Briefly mention any regulatory or approval requirements your product or service must meet. State who has jurisdiction and how you will satisfy these requirements.

Future Development Plans

Describe the nature and application of future development plans. Discuss whether these plans are improvements, and extension of the current product/service line or plans for other products/services. State whether these plans will address your current market or other markets. Discuss the timeframes for these plans. Justify why these plans are important by showing increased or newly generated profits.

Product Liability

Discuss the liability and insurance considerations that are inherent in manufacturing and/or marketing the product. Describe how you plan to limit the company's liability. Provide an estimate of the percent cost of the product that will be applied towards liability coverage.

Common Mistakes to Avoid

- The product/service description is too technical, too broad, or too ambiguous

- The section does not identify new, unique, or better capabilities, features, or benefits

- The homework is not done on protection availability or, not showing how to protect product/service from liability or competition

- The section identifies too much red tape and uncertainties from regulatory agencies

- Weak future development plans for improvements, expansion, staying ahead of market needs and competition

- Failure to consider the reliability, maintenance, and/or updating factors to keep "downtime" at a minimum

- Failure to include a third party evaluation of your product/service

LORD PUBLISHING, INC., 1988

Module 5 — Technology: Research and Development

Suggested Length   1–2 pages

Objective   To provide an overview of the unique technology your product utilizes. To outline the Research and Development phase and significant accomplishments.

Note: This Module is primarily for ventures that underwent, or are continuing to undergo an extensive R&D phase.

Pertinent Questions

1. When did you begin developing the product?

    _____

    _____

    _____

2. Where and under what conditions was research and development conducted?

    _____

    _____

    _____

    Under what supervision?

    _____

    _____

3. How many man hours are involved?

    _____

4. What instrumentation, chemicals, components, etc., are utilized in the product?

    _____

    _____

    _____

5. What are the costs (to date) to develop the product?

_____

_____

_____

How have you financed these costs?

_____

_____

_____

6. How much of the product is developed? (Check and describe)
   ☐ electronics
   ☐ mechanics
   ☐ casing
   ☐ packaging/aesthetics
   ☐ full working prototype (how many?)

_____

_____

_____

_____

7. Has the product undergone stress tests, safety tests and other reliability tests?

_____

_____

8. Have you applied for, or received, patent protection?

_____

_____

9. What are the regulatory requirements to manufacture, license or market the product?

_____

_____

_____

10. Do you plan to manufacture this product yourself, or license it to an existing manufacturer?

_____

_____

11. How does the technology compare to similar products?

_____

_____

_____

Is it state of the art?

_____

_____

More advanced than competitors?

_____

_____

12. When will research and development be completed?

_____

When will the product be ready for mass production?

_____

When will the product be ready to be marketed and distributed?

_____

What R & D still needs to be done?

_____

_____

13. What contacts have you made concerning the research and development of this product?

_____

_____

Results?
- ☐ potential customers
- ☐ government agencies
- ☐ potential manufacturers, distributors
- ☐ potential investors

_____

_____

14. Who owns the concept, drawings, materials, marketing rights, etc.?

_____

_____

Give a breakdown of each and percent of ownership

_____

_____

_____

15. What have you learned through R & D?

_____

_____

_____

☐ technology transfer to other applications

_____

_____

☐ spinoff products

_____

_____

16. Have you tested the product in the marketplace? (Check and describe)
    ☐ ease of use, adaptability
    ☐ user acceptance
    ☐ instructions, training needed

_____

_____

_____

17. What have been the primary accomplishments and break-throughs?

_____

_____

_____

18. What have been the major risks, problems and setbacks?

_____

_____

_____

Subheadings to Include

Concept Development
Research, Testing, and Evaluation
Major Milestones and Breakthroughs
Current Status and Continuing R&D

What to Accomplish

Describe how the idea came about. Discuss how you developed the product from the idea stage through to a viable business opportunity. Highlight what you learned in the process and what still needs to be done to move the product into the marketplace.

The following is a suggested sequence of presentation:

Concept Development

Describe how the product came about. Discuss how long it has been in development and the related cost factors. Describe the initial concept and how it has changed and improved through the development process. Discuss any new applications or opportunities that have resulted. State who owns what portion of the concept and/or product and give the percentages of each. Describe the technology employed in development.

Research, Testing, and Evaluation

Describe all related research, testing, and evaluation activities. Mention any surveys, articles, or studies that may have been published as a result of these activities. Present your findings as factual conclusions and document them as supporting materials in your appendix. State what makes the product reliable. Discuss the results of your research in terms of production needs, cost factors, time requirements, documentation, maintenance, and updating requirements. Describe the facilities, conditions, instrumentation, and supervision with which the research was conducted.

Major Milestones and Breakthroughs

Discuss the significant milestones and accomplishments that were achieved during R&D. State when, and under what circumstances, the breakthroughs happened. Describe what impact they had or will have on the venture. Discuss how the technology or process is different or superior to similar products. Describe what risks and problems were overcome to reach these milestones.

Current Status and Continuing R&D

Discuss where the project stands now. Describe how much of the product has been developed and what still needs to be done to protect, manufacture, license, market, and/or distribute it. Discuss how much of this you will be involved in doing or who may take over the development of these things. State when R&D will be completed. Discuss what contacts you have made regarding the product and the results of the contacts.

Common Mistakes to Avoid

- Superficial investigation or development; overlooking or not recognizing fundamental problems or flaws

- Inadequate testing; not fully evaluating potential short-comings or failures by not developing adequate test procedures and conditions

- Lack of certified test where applicable; trying to establish creditability of results with insufficient data and standards

- Inadequate safety considerations — shielding, isolation, grounding, types of materials used, etc.

- Lack of attention to reliability factors; failure to define, test, and evaluate reliability considerations

- Lack of plan for future development and manufacturing; inadequate consideration of manufacturing requirements and materials; lack of drawings and specifications

- Over designing; failure to observe the KIS Principle (Keep It Simple)

- Comparing technology you are involved with now with the technology the competition has now, even though you won't have it on the market for a year or two (the competition's technology and advances will have changed by then)

Module 6 — Market Analysis

Suggested Length   3–5 pages

Objective   To demonstrate that you understand the market, that you can penetrate it, and that you are in control of the critical success factors which will enable the company to reach its sales goals. Above all, to prove there is a demand for your product/service.

Pertinent Questions
1. Who or what is your target market? (Check and describe)

   ☐ individuals

   ☐ companies (small, medium, large)

   ☐ government agencies

   ☐ other _____

   _____

   _____

   _____

   _____

2. What is the size of your target market?

   _____

   _____

3. Can this market be segmented (by geography, by industries, etc.)? How?

   _____

   _____

   _____

   _____

LORD PUBLISHING, INC., 1988

4. What is the profile of your targeted customers?

   age _____

   sex _____

   profession _____

   income _____

   geographic location _____

   other demographics _____

   _____

   _____

   _____

   _____

5. What are the major applications of your product or service?

   _____

   _____

   _____

   _____

6. For each major application, what are the requirements by customers?

   _____

   _____

   _____

   What are the requirements of regulatory agencies?

   _____

   _____

   What are the current ways of filling these requirements?

   _____

   _____

   What are the buying habits of the customers?

   _____

   _____

   _____

7. What will be the impact (economic or otherwise) on the customers who use your product or service?

_____

_____

_____

How much will they save?

_____

_____

What is their return on investment (benefits)?

_____

_____

Will they have to change their way of doing things?

_____

_____

_____

Will they have to purchase other goods and services to utilize yours?

_____

_____

Will they have to change their work habits?

_____

_____

Overall, how will you satisfy their needs or wants better?

_____

_____

_____

_____

8. What share of the market do you hope to capture?

_____

_____

9. What is the growth (historical and potential) of your market?

_____

_____

What are the market trends?

_____

_____

_____

_____

Is the market seasonal?

_____

_____

_____

_____

What factors will affect it (economic, government regulation, etc.)?

_____

_____

_____

10. What are your market share objectives for the total available market?

_____

What are your market share objectives for the service available market?

_____

What are your market share objectives for the replacement market?

_____

11. What is your rationale and costs of achieving different levels of penetration?

_____

_____

_____

_____

12. How will you maintain and increase your market share?

_____

_____

_____

_____

LORD PUBLISHING, INC., 1988

How will you satisfy current customer needs?

_____

_____

_____

_____

How will you attract new customers?

_____

_____

_____

_____

How will you offer something new, better, or unique?

_____

_____

_____

_____

13. How will the segments and applications of your market change over the next 3-5 years?

_____

_____

_____

_____

14. Are your product/services bought by others to service their customers?

_____

_____

How does their industry look? What kind of business are they doing?

_____

_____

_____

15. How will you distribute your product? (Check and describe)

☐ direct

☐ dealer network

☐ wholesale

☐ retail

☐ manufacturers representatives

☐ other _____

_____

_____

_____

_____

Will it be distributed under your name or someone else's?

_____

_____

16. If transportation is involved, what are the implications of exporting? importing? taxes? tariffs? duties? barriers? foreign exchange and other concerns?

_____

_____

_____

_____

17. Have you received reactions from prospective customers?

_____

What was their reaction?

_____

_____

Have they tested a realistic prototype?

_____

_____

18. Are your sales expectations in line with the manufacturing ability to produce it?

_____

_____

19. Are your pricing, service, and warranty policies attractive and competitive in the marketplace?

_____

_____

20. What does each product/service cost you to sell?

_____

_____

What does each product/service cost you to produce?

_____

_____

_____

21. What have (will) your profits been (be) by product/service?

_____

_____

_____

22. What are your current sales goals by product/service?

_____

_____

What are your current sales goals by number of units?

_____

_____

What is your sales volume in dollars?

_____

_____

_____

_____

Subheadings to Include

Target Market and Characteristics
Analyst Summaries
Market Share, Trends, and Growth Potential
Sales, Distribution, and Profits by Product/Service
Service and Warranty Policies

What to Accomplish   Citing facts from your research and experience, show why and how your company will be successful. Most importantly, prove there is a market for your product/service and that your potential share and resulting profit projections are realistic.

The following is a suggested sequence of presentation:

Target Market and Characteristics

Describe your target market, who or what, and give a profile. Discuss how your product/service meets the needs/wants of this market. Discuss the "buying" record and habits of your customers. State pertinent facts concerning the size, age, location/area, profession, income, and other demographic information about the market. Allude to any self performed or professional research, studies, or surveys conducted. Include a list of these in a biography in the Appendices.

Analyst Summaries

Provide a series of quotes and statements that summarize significant facts, figures, and trends about the *market* (and market potential) from various reputable sources. Make sure you properly credit the source and provide the date of publication. The objective is to pinpoint specific market opportunities that exist within the industry, and how your products/services capitalize on these opportunities. The quotes and statements should make it clear what problems and needs exist in your market. It should become evident to the reader that your products/services can solve these problems and/or meet these needs better than existing methods.

Market Share, Trends, and Growth Potential

State the percent share of the market you now have or hope to penetrate. Discuss the trends of the market; industry wide, regional, and local. State if the market is seasonal, the timeframes, and how you will adjust and compensate during the off-season. Discuss how the market may change over the next 3–5 years. Discuss the growth potential of the entire market and your increased share. State on what assumptions you base these growth patterns (i.e., technology development, changing customer needs, costs, etc.). Discuss your rationale and the costs and risks associated with achieving higher levels of penetration.

Sales, Distribution, and Profits by Product/Service

Discuss your projected sales record by product/service. State what each product/service costs you to produce, distribute, and sell. Discuss how your product/service will be distributed and sold. Describe any unique features of your sales and distribution network. Discuss the implications of transportation, tariffs, duties, foreign exchange, and other government regulations.

Common Mistakes to Avoid

- Believing that the size of the market (customer) base is equally distributed (for example, your total market may be North Dakota, but the majority of your sales may come from the eastern part of the state)

- Failure to prove that your target market represents the major portion of the demand for your product/service (80/20 rule – 20 percent of the customers may represent 80 percent of the demand)

- Unrealistic market share projections (believing you can capture 100 percent of the market)

- Failure to demonstrate a clear understanding of the product/service to be sold and to what market

- No accurate estimate of the profitability of each product/service

- Basing sales projections on a higher degree of output than you have adequately demonstrated can actually be met

- Pricing not in line with target market needs, desires, or ability to pay

- Not properly assessing the total market potential, or changes in the market caused by economic, social, or other trends

- Not supporting your target market assumptions in light of advances in technology, government regulations, population shifts, and economic forces (oil prices, interest rates, etc.)

- Addressing (attacking) your market universally; not segmenting your market into various components and developing profiles of each; defining your market too broadly

- Presenting your facts to make your market appear subservient to your company's needs instead of vice versa

Module 7 — Competitive Analysis

Suggested Length   2–3 pages

Objective   To show that you are fully aware of the competitive forces at work in your marketplace. To explain your strengths over the competition, how you will counteract their advantages and overcome or compensate for your weaknesses.

Pertinent Questions

1. Who are your nearest and largest major competitors?

    _____

    _____

    _____

    _____

2. Is their business steady, increasing, or decreasing?

    _____

    _____

    _____

    Why?

    _____

    _____

    _____

3. How does your business compare to your competitors' (strengths and weaknesses of each)?

    ☐ in length of time in business?

    ☐ in sales volume (units and dollars)?

    ☐ in size and number of employees, suppliers, and support personnel?

    ☐ in number of customers? share of market? product niche?

    _____

    _____

    _____

    _____

4. What are the similarities/dissimilarities between your business and your competitors' business?

   _____

   _____

   _____

   _____

5. On what basis will you compete with them? (Check and describe)

   ☐ product superiority

   ☐ price

   ☐ advertising

   ☐ technology/innovation

   ☐ other _____

   _____

   _____

   _____

   _____

6. In what aspect(s) is your business better? (What is your distinctive competence?). (Check and describe)

   ☐ operations

   ☐ management

   ☐ product

   ☐ price

   ☐ service

   ☐ delivery

   ☐ other _____

   _____

   _____

   _____

   _____

7. What have you learned by observing your competition?

   _____

   _____

   _____

   _____

8. What competition will you meet in each product/service line?

_____

_____

_____

_____

9. How does your product/service compare with the competition in the eyes of customers?

_____

_____

_____

_____

10. What do you know about others like you, not yet in the market?

_____

_____

_____

11. If you have no competition, what kind (who) might you create by being successful in the marketplace?

_____

_____

_____

12. Do you threaten the major strategic objectives or self image of the competition?

_____

_____

Will you seriously affect their profits? (Will they attempt to destroy you at any cost?)

_____

_____

_____

Subheadings to Include	Competitors Profile Product/Services Comparison Market Niche and Share Comparison of Strengths and Weaknesses
What to Accomplish	Give a brief run-down on the other industry participants. Highlight your particular competitive edge.

The following is a suggested sequence of presentation:

Competitors' Profile

Discuss the competition: size, age, locations, sales volume, management, mode of operation, and other characteristics. Discuss potential competitors who may enter your market.

Product/Service Comparison

Discuss the similarities and differences between your product/service and that of the competition. Compare your operations and management style with your various competitors. Highlight whatever it is that makes your product/service and company more attractive in the marketplace.

Market Niche and Share

State the approximate percentages each of your competitors' holds in the market. Discuss those that hold the large percentages and why they have an edge. Discuss the competitors who have/are coming on strong and are making (or expected to make) bigger gains in the market. Discuss the particular segments of the market that each of your competitors addresses. Discuss your niche in relation to these and what percent of the total market it makes up. Describe where the market is headed and how each competitor's niche and share may change over the next 3–5 years.

Comparison of Strengths and Weaknesses

Discuss your strengths and weaknesses in relation to your major competitors. It is helpful to list the variables down the left-hand column and the competition and your company along the top of the page. The reader can quickly summarize the characteristics, as well as the strengths and weaknesses of all participants at a glance. The major strengths and weaknesses you should summarize are: product superiority, price advantages, market advantages (large contracts with customers or suppliers, proximity to a larger market, proximity of labor supplies, raw materials, energy, transportation, land or other resources) and finally, management strengths and weaknesses (experience and track record, skills, etc.).

Common Mistakes to Avoid:

- Not identifying known major competitors

- Underestimating competitive strength and potential

- Failure to demonstrate your competitive edge — what makes you unique or better

- Having no strategy for counteracting current competition or emerging competition

- Assuming you have no competition

- Failure to show an awareness of competitors' plans in the market and their business cycles.

Module 8 — Marketing Strategy

Suggested Length	2–3 pages
Objective	To explain specifically how you will enter the market, obtain a niche, maintain a market share, and achieve the stated financial projections.
Pertinent Questions	1. What is the sales appeal of your product/service?

_____

_____

_____

What is special or unique about it?

_____

_____

_____

_____

2. How will you attract and maintain your market?

_____

_____

_____

_____

How will you expand it?

_____

_____

_____

Over what period of time?

_____

_____

_____

3. What are your marketing priorities among segments and applications? (You can't be all things to all people, regardless of the opportunity.)

_____

_____

_____

4. How will you identify prospective customers?

_____

_____

_____

_____

5. How will you reach the decision makers?

_____

_____

_____

_____

6. How will you decide whom to contact?

_____

_____

_____

_____

In what order?

_____

_____

_____

7. What level of selling effort will you implement?

_____

_____

_____

Why is this the best approach?

_____

_____

_____

How many salesmen? In-house staff or manufacturer's representatives?

_____

_____

_____

_____

How much direct mail and brochure distribution?

_____

_____

_____

_____

How many trade shows? which ones?

_____

_____

_____

_____

8. What advertising/promotion mediums will you use? (Check and describe)
   - ☐ radio
   - ☐ newspaper
   - ☐ trade journals
   - ☐ magazines
   - ☐ television

_____

_____

_____

_____

9. What are your efficiency ratios and conversion rates?

_____

_____

_____

How many calls are made per demonstration?

_____

_____

How many demonstrations per sale?

_____

_____

How much direct mail and expected response rate?

_____

_____

How many other media ads and expected response rate?

_____

_____

10. How long will the above activities take?

_____

_____

_____

11. What will each customer's average order size be?

_____

_____

What kind of repeat orders can you expect?

_____

_____

12. What are the quotas and sales productivity of each salesperson?

_____

_____

_____

What is the commission structure?

_____

_____

What is the sales cycle?

_____

_____

What are the milestones for meeting sales expectations?

_____

_____

_____

13. What geographic areas will be covered?

_____

_____

_____

14. What will your pricing strategy be?

_____

_____

Will your margins be low or high?

_____

_____

_____

What will your discount policy be?

_____

_____

_____

What will your dealer margins be?

_____

_____

_____

15. How may pricing change over time?

_____

_____

How may pricing change after recouping R & D costs?

_____

_____

What about possible pricing wars with competition?

_____

_____

What are the critical supply and demand factors?

_____

_____

_____

16. How will your packaging and labeling enhance name identification and foster brand loyalty? (Why will a prospective customer want to buy your product just by seeing it?)

_____

_____

_____

17. What will your credit and collection policies be?

_____

_____

18. What kind (and level) of service, warranties and guarantees will you offer?

_____

_____

How will you promote these?

_____

_____

How may these affect profits?

_____

_____

Subheadings to Include

Market Penetration Goals
Pricing and Packaging
Sales and Distribution
Service and Warranty Policies
Advertising, Public Relations, and Promotions

What to Accomplish

Describe your plan of action for being successful in the market. Discuss how your internal policies and your utilization of the media will contribute to that success. Reference your Marketing Plan if you have developed one independently of the Business Plan.

The following is a suggested sequence of presentation:

Market Penetration Goals

Describe your plans for entering the market. State what your estimated sales and share will be. Discuss the sales appeal among specific segments of the market. Discuss how you will identify prospective customers within each segment, how you will prioritize them, and how you will reach them. State your timetables for achieving these penetration goals and how your strategy may be affected by the reactions of competitors. Discuss any major customers who you have precommitted and how they may help you to further penetrate the market.

LORD PUBLISHING, INC., 1988

Pricing and Packaging

Describe your pricing policies and how they are determined. Discuss the influences of the competition, discounts, cost of goods, market forces and other factors that will affect pricing. Justify your prices, particularly if they ar substantially above or below the prices of similar products/services in the marketplace. Above all, demonstrate that your pricing decision is based on your company's ability to make a profit.

Discuss your packaging and labeling design plans. Describe how the brand name, colors, logo and overall packaging appeal will entice customers to buy. Discuss the directions or instructions that accompany the product and how you make the product easy to use.

Sales and Distribution

Discuss any relationships you have with suppliers and/or distributors. Mention any distribution or licensing agreements that are in force or that you are seeking. Describe how your product/service will be distributed and over what geographical area. Discuss the method(s) of sales and retailing, direct sales and other methods. Discuss how these will be attracted, compensated and controlled.

Discuss your selling arrangements in terms of cash sales, financing, leasing, credit and payment terms. If you will be employing salesmen, discuss their quotas and incentives. (Remember that sales volume will be directly proportional to the number of effective sales calls made. Prospective investors will want to see you knocking on doors). Discuss briefly your hiring, training and promotion program.

Service and Warranty Policies

Describe your service arrangements, product support, warranty terms and customer orientation of these things. Discuss how these policies make you competitive and how they may affect profits. Discuss the procedures for implementing these policies. State how they are reviewed by management and how they may change or be improved upon as you gain experience. Describe how you will handle customer complaints and other problems with product/service.

Advertising, Public Relations and Promotions

Describe your advertising, public relations and promotional programs and campaigns. Discuss the mediums you will use and any professional ad agencies you may retain. Describe your overall approach and strategy for introducing your product/service and gaining its market familiarity and acceptance. Discuss how the company's name, or the product/service name may contribute to market identity. Discuss your attendance at conventions and trade shows within the industry the industry.

Common Mistakes to Avoid

- Discussing "marketing" and "sales" in the same terms: ("Sales" is dealing directly with your customers; it is a developed art form. "Marketing" is enticing them to consider your product; it is an acquired discipline)

- Justifying your prices by the cost to produce, market and/or sell your product/service. (Sales price is a function of value in the eyes of your customers only. Too low a price is as detrimental as too high a price.)

- Assuming that your sales, efforts, whether in house or factory direct network, can be set up with minimal time and expense (It takes as much as one year for salesperson to get acquainted with a product and learn a territory.) Start-up ventures should investigate using established agent/representative/distributor network; the learning curve and amount of time to establish is much shorter

- Assuming your distribution network will give your product/service equal "sales" time, if you do use an independent agent or representative

- Failure to promote marketable differences in your product over the competition

- Attempting to immediately fill several lucrative, but unrelated market gaps

- Strategy too broad, not rational or achievable

- Underestimating the importance of packaging and brand name

Module 9 — Manufacturing/Process/Operations

Suggested Length   3-5 pages

Objective   To explain how you will produce your product in a cost efficient way and ready it for the market.

Pertinent Questions

1. How will you accomplish production (or conduct service operations)?

_____
_____
_____
_____

2. How much will you do internally?

_____
_____
_____

By what methods?

_____
_____
_____

3. How much of production will be accomplished through subcontracts?

_____
_____

Initially?

_____
_____

After two or three years?

_____
_____

LORD PUBLISHING, INC., 1988

4. What materials and components are required for production?

_____

_____

What are the critical parts?

_____

_____

5. Who/what are the sources of supply for these parts?

_____

_____

Are any of these parts sole sourced?

_____

_____

Do you have back-up vendors or alternatives should materials or suppliers become unavailable?

_____

_____

What are the lead times of these parts?

_____

_____

6. Are production facilities and equipment leased or purchased?

_____

_____

What is the condition of the facilities and equipment?

_____

_____

Are there any liens on the property or equipment?

_____

Have you done a title search?

_____

7. What is your planned capacity for level of production or operations?

_____

_____

In dollars?

_____

_____

In units?

_____

_____

How may this be expanded?

_____

_____

What are the production cycles?

_____

_____

_____

8. What are the standard costs for production at different volume levels? (breakdown of fixed and variable costs)

_____

_____

_____

9. What are your plans for equipment set-up and facility layout so production flows with a minimum of problems and bottlenecks?

_____

_____

_____

10. In planning facility and equipment layout, have you considered: future expansion needs/plans?

_____

_____

output capacity — will it meet peak demand, or meet lower levels of demand and stockpile inventory?

_____

_____

space requirements for restrooms, office, storage, receiving, manufacturing, lounge, other?

_____

_____

11. Will the plant be set up for process layout (machines grouped by function) or production layout (machines grouped according to the needs of the product being manufactured)?

_____

_____

_____

12. Have you determined the order in which jobs will be done at each workstation? (Check and describe)

   ☐ first come/first served

   ☐ shortest operation time (SOT), first served

   ☐ last in, first served

   ☐ other _____

   _____

   _____

   _____

   _____

13. Have you separated the cost to produce each unit by material and labor?

_____

_____

Have you figured the indirect costs; i.e. supplies, utilities, management and clerical salaries, insurance, taxes, depreciation, interest, etc.?

_____

_____

_____

What is the breakeven point?

_____

_____

_____

_____

14. What are your other production control procedures?

_____

_____

_____

What is your safety record and procedures?

_____

_____

_____

15. What is your quality control system?

_____

_____

_____

_____

_____

16. What are your inventory control considerations?

_____

_____

_____

What is your level of "buffer stock" needed to absorb random variations in demand?

_____

_____

_____

What kind of fixed order or cycle order inventory system will you implement?

_____

_____

_____

What is the shelf life of the product?

_____

_____

_____

17. What are your labor considerations?

_____

_____

_____

What are the effects of possible strikes/union activity?

_____

_____

_____

What are the training needs?

_____

_____

_____

What are the effects of changes in compensation/productivity, structure or quotas?

_____

_____

_____

18. How will you make the most effective use of your labor pool?

_____

_____

_____

Can your personnel handle more than one machine or function?

_____

_____

19. What is the potential environmental impact of your plant location or manufacturing process, in terms of:
    restrictions? licenses? zoning?
    disposal of waste?
    pollution and noise control?
    other considerations?

_____

_____

_____

_____

20. What are the advantages and disadvantages of your present or planned location, in terms of:
proximity to customers?
proximity to labor, suppliers, capital?
access to transportation, energy, utilities, (rates) and other resources?
state and local laws (zoning, regulation, etc.)

_____

_____

_____

21. What are the characteristics of your location in terms of size?

_____

_____

_____

What are the characteristics of your location in terms of structure?

_____

_____

_____

What are the characteristics of your location in terms of surrounding (is the area stable, changing, improving, deteriorating)?

_____

_____

_____

22. What short-term or long-range plans do you have/need for the facility and location?

_____

_____

_____

What short-term or long-range plans do you have/need for renovations and costs?

_____

_____

_____

What short-term or long range plans do you have/need for additional features or replacement fixtures?

_____

_____

_____

What short-term or long-range plans do you have/nned for a new location?

_____

_____

_____

23. How does your location affect your operating costs?

_____

_____

_____

24. What other businesses (kinds) are in the area?

_____

_____

_____

_____

25. What will be the costs and timing of any acquisitions?

_____

_____

_____

_____

26. Overall, what production or operating advantages do you have?

_____

_____

_____

_____

27. What economic impact may your plant location, and business in general, have on the community in which your will be located? (Check and describe)
    ☐ job creation
    ☐ improving the sales of area suppliers
    ☐ existing companies relocating to the area, or spurring new companies
    ☐ other _____

_____

_____

_____

_____

Subheadings to Include

Location
Facilities and Equipment
Manufacturing Process and Operations
Labor Considerations
Environmental and Economic Impact

What to Accomplish

Demonstrate you have a good handle on all aspects of your company's manufacturing process and operations. This is where most business plans fall short, because it is the area that causes most businesses to fail. This is where the major costs and headaches of a company are found. You want to show you have given these issues serious thought. Describe how you will minimize the cost and inherent problems of manufacturing, while maximizing profits through efficient operations.

The following is a suggested sequence of presentation:

Location

Describe your company's location, or proposed location. State if the land will be purchased, leased, or rented. Describe the surrounding area and other types of businesses in the neighborhood. Discuss the advantages and disadvantages of your location in terms of proximity to customers or markets; availability of labor, suppliers, and capital; access to transportation, energy, utilities, and other resources. Discuss the state and local laws such as zoning, licenses, and other regulations that may affect your company. Highlight the favorable climate that exists in and around the location. Discuss how your location will affect your operating costs. Finally, state whether your long range plans and needs call for you to remain where you are, or move to establish a new location.

Environmental and Economic Impact

Describe how your company and its manufacturing operations will impact the environment and the community. Discuss how you will dispose of waste; apply for applicable licenses; be affected by other restrictions, such as pollution and noise control. Highlight the economic benefits that will result from your business operating in the community. Discuss the "trickle down" effect of your business boosting others, creating jobs, etc.

Facilities and Equipment

Describe the characteristics of the facilities in terms of size, structure, and condition. Describe the kind of equipment used in your manufacturing operations and its condition. State whether the facilities and equipment are purchased, leased, or rented. Discuss any special parts or needs that must accompany the facilities and equipment. Discuss the maintenance and replacement requirements of the facilities and equipment. Highlight how and why the facilities and equipment give you better production or operating advantages over similar businesses. Finally, discuss the long-range needs and plans for your facilities and equipment.

Manufacturing Process and Operations

Describe how you will manufacture and produce your product, and/or conduct service operations. Discuss the methods and processes involved. State how much of this will be done internally and how much will be subcontracted. Discuss how internal operations or subcontracting relationships may change over the next few years. Describe the raw materials and/or components used in producing your product. Discuss how these are supplied and your back-up system should your primary suppliers become unavailable.

State your current, or initial projected capacity for level of production or operations in dollars and in units. Discuss how this may be expanded or changed in any other way. Break down the fixed and variable costs of production and operations at different volume levels. Describe the costs to produce each unit by material and labor. Include the indirect costs (utilities, taxes, insurance, etc.) and show the break-even point.

Describe the product/operations layout (a sample in included in this guide's appendix). Discuss workflow and production control procedures. Discuss your safety program, quality control, and inventory control systems. Show how they are conducive to a positive and productive work environment, and are cost effective as well.

Labor Considerations

Discuss what labor requirements you will have; how you will hire and train them. Discuss how you will handle the possibility of strikes and other labor union activities. Discuss how you will minimize turnovers, structure compensation, productivity quotas, and employee benefits. Discuss how you will handle discipline cases and how you will communicate company policies as they relate to infractions and expectations.

Common Mistakes to Avoid

■ Failure to properly assess the manufacturing process, operations and alternative methods, in terms of their costs (taxes, freight, and installation, maintenance, etc.), production capabilities, serviceability, delivery times, and other considerations

■ Not adequately identifying or providing for ancillary needs and equipment, such as special drainage requirement, ventilation systems, fixtures, etc.)

■ Improperly planning for efficient plant layout, materials handling, work spaces, travel, and other considerations

■ Poor scheduling of work force, hiring and layoff, overtime, additional shifts, subcontracting and inventories

■ Not optimizing the combination of available capacities to meet demand and hold down costs

■ Poor inventory control planning. No balance between meeting customer demand and minimizing associated costs, i.e., ordering production, handling and storage, capital allocations, shortages, etc.

■ Failure to maintain proper inventory levels; inadequate inventory control system; inadequate controls in monitoring purchasing function

■ Failure to identify and account for all product costs (fixed, variable, indirect)

■ Poor personnel management and hiring practices; poor attention to selection process, training, pay scales and benefits, union influences, and explanation of company policies and expectations

■ Underestimating the environmental (especially as it pertains to regulations) and economic impact

■ Failing to plan for long-range needs and changes in location, facility, and equipment

LORD PUBLISHING, INC., 1988

Module 10 — Management and Ownership

Suggested Length   2–3 pages

Objective   To demonstrate that the management and leadership is capable, fairly compensated, and given every incentive to be successful. To show the ownership distribution, who they are, and how much they own.

Pertinent Questions   1. Who are your key managers?

_____

_____

_____

_____

2. What is the personal history of each principal?
age
educational background (formal and informal)
talents, skills, abilities
health
outside interests

_____

_____

_____

_____

_____

3. What does each principal bring to this venture?
number of years direct experience in industry
track record
length of time with this project
business/management background

_____

_____

_____

_____

_____

4. What is the position and role of each principal?
   title
   responsibilities, duties, and/or overlapping functions

   _____

   _____

   _____

   _____

5. What is the compensation package of each principal?
   salary
   profit sharing
   bonuses and other fringe benefits
   terms of employment

   _____

   _____

   _____

   _____

6. What is the ownership interest of each principal?

   _____

   _____

   _____

   _____

7. Who is on the Board of Directors?
   inside representation
   outside representation
   age
   corporate affiliation
   compensation
   ownership
   special contributions

   _____

   _____

   _____

   _____

   _____

   _____

8. What is the primary objective of the current owners and managers? (Check and describe)

☐ sellout in x number of years

☐ buy out investors

☐ license idea for royalties

☐ franchise idea

☐ other _____

_____

_____

_____

_____

_____

9. How do you intend to attract and compensate additional key people as the company grows?

_____

_____

_____

_____

10. Do any of your people have outstanding "noncompete" agreements with previous employers?

_____

_____

_____

Do they have one with you?

_____

_____

Have you obtained legal advice on their validity and applicability?

_____

_____

_____

11. Has the loss of a key member of your team been considered from a tax planning standpoint, from a knowledge, information and learning curve perspective and from a management succession point of view

_____

_____

_____

12. Is there a written succession plan?

_____

_____

13. How much life insurance is being carried on key personnel where the company is the beneficiary?

_____

_____

_____

14. What is the amount of stock currently authorized and issued?

_____

_____

15. Who are your current stockholders?

_____

_____

_____

_____

How many shares does each own?

_____

_____

_____

What are the warrants, right, options?

_____

_____

_____

16. What about you?
    What is your reason for going into business?

    _____

    _____

    _____

    _____

    Are you physically suited to do the job?

    _____

    _____

    _____

17. Who is on your professional team? (Check and describe)
    ☐ lawyer
    ☐ accountant
    ☐ banker
    ☐ tax specialist
    ☐ trade association
    ☐ consultants (marketing, management, systems, etc.)

    _____

    _____

    _____

    _____

Subheadings to Include

Management
Board of Directors
Ownership
Professional Support Resources

What to Accomplish

Show that your company has proper balance. Having too many marketing and sales type people in management is as bad as having too many bean counters (finance people) making the critical decisions. Demonstrate adequate expertise in all areas of marketing, management, technical finance, manufacturing, etc. Show you have recruited in the areas where you personally are weak. Above all, differentiate between ownership and management roles, even if they are assumed by the same individuals.

The following is a suggested sequence of presentation:

Management

Discuss your management team. Give a brief background of the principals (decision makers). Describe each principal's distinctive competence and what they bring to the company. Discuss education, experience, knowledge of industry, special talents, training, skills, and abilities.

Discuss each principal's position, duties, and responsibilities. State how long they have been with the project and any significant accomplishments with the company. Discuss each principal's compensation package i.e.; salary, profit sharing, bonuses and incentives, fringe benefits, and other terms of employment. State what each principal's objective is with the company; i.e., what they want to get out of their involvement, short term or long range. Discuss any noncompete agreements or other legal contracts that each has executed with the company.

If all the management positions have not yet been filled, describe the qualifications that will be needed in a person to fill these positions. State how and when you expect to recruit additional key people. Discuss how you intend to attract and compensate them. Along these lines, describe any positions that may be created as your company grows.

Describe what options or alternatives you may pursue if you lose a key person. State what your own personal plans are for grooming a successor. Discuss how you will minimize the negative impacts of losing or having to fire key managers.

Allude to the resumes and personal references from customers, suppliers, bankers, former employers, etc., on each of your key people that are included as supporting documents in your plans appendix.

Board of Directors

Discuss who is on your Board of Directors and why they are valuable to the business. State what their field of expertise is and their other corporate affiliations. Describe any special contributions they have already made, or are expected to make. State how the Board is compensated for their time and advice, how often they meet, and how much control or influence they wield.

If you have not yet recruited a Board of Directors, describe the kind of individuals you would like to place, how and when you expect to recruit them.

Ownership

Give a breakdown of the ownership interest of all parties; who owns what and how much. Describe the form of ownership; i.e., stock, partnership percentages, notes, etc. State the type of ownership, i.e., preferred stock, common stock, straight debt, debt with warrants, convertible debentures, etc.

Discuss the amount and kind of ownership in reserve (not yet issued). Discuss how the ownership breakdown may change by taking on additional managers and/or capital from investors. Describe the proposed distribution of ownership if not yet firm.

Discuss any plans or agreements you have pertaining to buy outs, dissolution of company, managers/owners leaving the company and other possible developments. Discuss the warrants, privileges, rights and options of all current and future owners.

If you are seeking financing through this business plan, allude to personal financial statements included in the Appendix.

Professional Support Resources

Describe your support team and how each has, or will, assist in the development and ongoing management of your company. A partial list may include: lawyer, accountant, banker, tax specialist, trade association affiliation, public relations consultant, marketing/advertising consultant, technical/systems consultant, etc.

If you have not yet used consultants, show the reader you are aware of the support services your company may need. Discuss which professional you may use and when they would come into play.

Common Mistakes to Avoid

- Having friends, relatives, or other people in key management positions who are not qualified for specialized functions

- Wanting the reader to assume that a successful manager from a different industry will be successful in your company's industry

- Failure to protect the proprietary nature of your product or confidentiality of your operations by not having key people sign noncompete agreements and/or employment contracts

- Offering particular people too much ownership or other compensation because you are desperate to attract and keep good people (base your incentives on achieving milestones so that key people will pay for themselves)

- Failure to identify and recruit a prestigious and active Board of Directors

- Demonstrating an unwillingness to step aside after the company outgrows your entrepreneurial inspiration and requires more of a maintenance type manager

- Not having a succession plan or crisis management plan in the event of unexpectedly losing key people

- Failure to provide for reserve ownership for use in second-round financing, attracting additional Board members or management, with a minimum of hassle from current owners

- Locking into wrong type ownership, in light of tax benefits, dividend disbursement or other priorities of current or future owners

- Failure to provide for advice, counsel, and support services of needed professionals

Module 11 — Administration, Organization, and Personnel

Suggested Length   1–2 pages

Objective   To show control and efficiency of standard administrative functions. To outline the company organization, lines of authority, and responsibility. To give a sketch of your staffing needs.

Pertinent Questions
1. What is your organizational structure? (Include an organization chart.)

_____

_____

_____

Does everyone know who reports/answers to whom?

_____

_____

_____

Are clear lines of authority and responsibility established?

_____

_____

2. Do you have a bookkeeping system set up?

_____

_____

_____

3. What are your administrative policies, procedures, and controls for billings, payments and accounts receivable?

_____

_____

_____

What are your administrative policies, producedures, and controls for management reporting?

_____

_____

_____

What are your administrative policies, procedures, and controls for employee training, probation periods, promotions, incentives, discipline, etc.?

_____

_____

_____

What are your administrative policies, procedures, and controls for travel, phone usage, supplies, car allowance and other expenses?

_____

_____

_____

4. What are your management philosophies and style?

_____

_____

_____

_____

_____

_____

How will you motivate employees (incentives)?

_____

_____

_____

_____

How will you create a positive work environment?

_____

_____

_____

_____

How will you manage for goal attainment? (MBO — Management By Objectives)

_____

_____

_____

_____

How will you encourage creativity and entrepreneurship?

_____

_____

_____

_____

How will you foster commitment and loyalty in your employees?

_____

_____

_____

_____

5. What is your current (or initially planned) personnel make-up?
   number of employees
   skills
   seasonal hiring and layoff factors

_____

_____

_____

_____

_____

_____

6. What is your average or expected turnover?

_____

_____

_____

7. What are your personnel needs?
   6 months _____
   1 year _____
   3 years _____
   number of people needed _____
   skills _____
   full-time _____
   part-time _____

_____

_____

_____

8. Are the people you will need (level of knowledge, qualifications) available in the marketplace, or will you have to train?

_____

_____

_____

_____

9. How will you attract and compensate employees?
   by skill level
   by job class
   other _____

_____

_____

_____

_____

10. How do your personnel know where they stand?
    What are they supposed to do (job descriptions)?

_____

_____

_____

When are they supposed to do it?

_____

_____

_____

How are they supposed to do it?

_____

_____

_____

Expectations of management and prospects for advancement?

_____

_____

_____

_____

_____

11. Do you have periodic performance evaluations?

_____

_____

_____

12. What are the costs of these administrative functions?

_____

_____

_____

_____

Subheadings to Include

Organizational Chart
Administrative Procedures and Controls
Staffing and Training
Management and Control Systems

What to Accomplish

Your readers are going to want to know how the company is managed, as much as who is managing it. Demonstrate your awareness and understanding of the administrative details. Explain what personnel are needed, how you will fill and train these positions. Include an organization chart that illustrates the company's structure, lines of authority, responsibility and delegation. Finally, give a brief synopsis of your management style and systems for ensuring excellence.

The following is a suggested sequence of presentation:

Organizational Chart

Illustrate the lines of authority, responsibility, and delegation with a chart. Make it clear who answers to whom. Do not make these areas of accountability look too authoritarian or rigid. Allow for flexibility and overlap of duties if appropriate for your situation. The reader should be able to glance at the chart and get a clear understanding of the management and personnel structure of the company. A sample organizational chart can be found in this guide's Appendix.

Administrative Procedures and Controls

Describe your administrative systems, procedures and controls. Mention specifically how you will handle the accounting and bookkeeping functions. Discuss how you will monitor and audit customer payments, bills incurred by the company, and accounts receivable. State how you will track and control internal expenses and operating costs. Discuss any other major administrative systems that are a necessary function of your venture, such as ordering, collecting, receiving, organizing, filing, storing, disseminating and disposing of goods, services and/or information.

Staffing and Training

Discuss your current, or needed personnel and their functions. State how they complement one another. Describe the nature, length, and cost of training needed for employees. Discuss any present or planned employment contracts you expect to utilize and enforce. Describe how personnel are identified, attracted, hired, and compensated. State your current or planned number of employees and future provisions for growth. Describe the learning and experience curve for different positions and the amount of time before they are self-functioning and productive. Sample job descriptions may be included in your plan's Appendix.

Management Control Systems

Briefly summarize your management philosophies and style. Tie these in with how you will go about getting the most out of your people. Describe your plans to encourage group goals over individual goals. Discuss how you will prevent your team from stagnating or becoming too bogged down in the routine and predictable decisions. In general, discuss how you will keep the lines of communication open, encourage creativity and commitment to company goals; remain lean, flexible, and action oriented.

Common Mistakes to Avoid

- Poor or inadequate system of accounting and other business records

- Failure to have some preconceived notions on how to manage and encourage the best possible performance

- Not having enough personnel to accomplish the tasks at hand

- Being over staffed; too many people doing too little work

- No clear lines of authority or accountability; poor management control systems

- Inadequate planning for future staff needs in light of growth or other changes

- Poor training and orientation procedures for personnel

- Offering substandard compensation and incentives

- Top heavy management (too many Chiefs, not enough Indians)

- Failure to demonstrate company purpose and commitment to team goals (not showing what is good for the whole is good for the part)

Module 12 — Milestones, Schedule, and Strategic Planning

Suggested Length   1–2 pages

Objective   To outline major company objectives and explain how and when they will be achieved.

Pertinent Questions 1. What needs to be done to launch this venture?

_____

_____

_____

_____

What needs to be done to raise the capital?

_____

_____

_____

_____

What needs to be done to identify and penetrate the market?

_____

_____

_____

_____

What needs to be done to identify, recruit, place and train management and personnel?

_____

_____

_____

_____

_____

What needs to be done to locate the company, line up suppliers, etc.?

_____

_____

_____

_____

What needs to be done to go operational?

_____

_____

_____

_____

2. Who is going to do these things?

_____

_____

_____

_____

When are they expected to be completed?

_____

_____

_____

3. What are the critical milestones and junctures that must be reached to make other things happen?

_____

_____

_____

_____

4. Do you have a "timeline" chart that identifies these milestones with month/day/year for completion?

_____

_____

5. Have you done any strategic planning for the venture?

_____

_____

_____

_____

6. What professionals and consultants have your retained, (or will be needed), to keep you on schedule and help you reach your goals?

_____

_____

_____

_____

7. Do your goals reflect a 'real world' view, or hopeful thinking?

_____

_____

_____

Are your goals actually attainable within the timeframes you set down?

_____

_____

_____

_____

How will you assure their attainment with a minimal margin of error?

_____

_____

_____

_____

8. What will you do if/when you do not reach key milestones?

_____

_____

_____

_____

9. Do you have a unified and coordinated effort toward the attainment of these goals?

_____

_____

_____

_____

Subheadings to   Major Milestones
Include   Schedule
                            Strategic Planning

What to Accomplish   Demonstrate that you know what must be done and how you will
                            pursue these goals in a realistic way, within a reasonable timeframe.
                            Concentrate on the critical, or all important milestones. Summarize
                            the implications of not attaining these milestones, and what
                            alternatives you may then pursue. Your goals should be centered
                            around positioning and strengthening yourself in the marketplace
                            through strategic planning.

The following is a suggested sequence of presentation:

Major Milestones

Summarize the significant goals that you and your venture have
already reached. Describe how you attained them and what you
learned in the process. Discuss what needs to be done and what
must happen for you to be successful with the company. State who
is in charge of seeing these things accomplished. Refer the reader to
the timeline schedule for when these things are expected to be
completed. Describe why these goals and timeframes are realistic.
Finally, give an example of the teamwork and unified commitment
towards the attainment of these goals.

Schedule

Include a timeline chart. This chart is a schedule of significant
milestones and their priority for completion. The far left-hand
column indicates the day, month, and year for completion. The
second from the left column states the milestone or goal to be
completed. The third column from the left states who is charged
with the task of overseeing or completing the goal. The last column
states what options or alternatives may be pursued if the goal is not
attained.

There are several ways to present the milestones within the chart.
You may list them in order of priority or in order of importance. (The
two are not necessarily the same.) You may also list them in logical
order for completion. In other words, one must happen before the
other can be considered or reached.

A sample timeline chart is included in the Appendices.

Strategic Planning

This is normally a very difficult issue for an owner/manager to tackle. It takes quite a bit of foresight and expertise, combining academic techniques with past experience in the company/industry. As with all other issues in your plan, do not try to bluff or be afraid to admit that you don't have all the answers. Your best bet is to consult professionals in the field. Lacking the resources to get professional help, get together your partners, managers, staff, friends, and other people involved, and conduct a "brainstorming" session.

In a brainstorming session, no idea or comment is too remote. Creativity and openness is to be encouraged, without criticism or qualification. Have your team throw out ideas on all major aspects of your product/service; and operations. After all ideas are exhausted, prioritize, assign, and begin putting some direction toward their exploration.

You should strategize according to:

- learning/experience curve
- industry participants
- leadership/management style
- available resources
- security of information
- flexibility, simplicity
- new approaches, element of surprise

The biggest factor in formulating effective strategies, while avoiding ones with inherent risks and failure, is to have an honest assessment of your strengths and weaknesses and to ask the right questions. In writing this section of your business plan, make it clear to the reader you are indeed addressing the right questions.

Common Mistakes to Avoid

- Failure to identify and prioritize the really significant or critical milestones
- Inadequately describing how you will attain your goals and how is responsible for the task
- Milestones not realistic, given available resources and/or timeframes for completion
- Failure to offer alternative plans of action if and when major milestones are not reached within a designated time period
- Failure to look ahead and plan for ways to improve sales and operations
- Believing that everything will go according to schedule

Module 13 — The Critical Risks and Problems

Suggested Length   1–2 pages

Objective   To demonstrate your knowledge of inevitable or potential problems and risks; to show your willingness to face up to them and deal with them in a forthright manners.

Pertinent Questions

1. What are the inherent and potential problems, risks, and other negatives your business will/may be faced with?

_____

_____

_____

_____

_____

_____

_____

_____

_____

_____

_____

_____

_____

2. Is the company or any principals involved in any threatened or pending litigation or disciplinary action?

_____

_____

_____

3. Is the company facing any stringent regulatory requirements?

_____

_____

_____

LORD PUBLISHING, INC., 1988

4. Is the company facing legal liability or other insurance problems?

_____

_____

_____

_____

5. What can you do to avoid these problems?

_____

_____

_____

_____

6. When are they likely to occur?

_____

_____

_____

7. How will you deal with them as they arise?

_____

_____

_____

_____

8. How can you minimize their impact?

_____

_____

_____

_____

9. What can be learned from these problems?

_____

_____

_____

_____

10. How may you possibly turn these problems into opportunities?

_____

_____

_____

_____

Subheadings to Include	Summary of Major Problems Overcome
	Inevitable Risks and Problems
	Potential Risks and Problems
	Worst Case Scenarios

What to Accomplish

Address the negatives that exist or you think may develop. The reader, especially investors, will appreciate your integrity by giving them the full story. Counteract the downside by describing how you plan to avoid, minimize, or turn around the major problems and risks.

The following is a suggested sequence of presentation:

Summary of Major Problems Overcome

Start by summarizing the major problems you have already had to deal with. Give examples of how you attacked and resolved these. Highlight especially innovative and creative approaches you have used to solve problems in your startup and what was learned from addressing these problems.

Inevitable Risks and Problems

Describe the nature of the problems and risks that you venture will be faced with. Discuss when these problems and risks are expected to present themselves. Discuss how you may avoid or minimize their impact. Describe how you will deal with them. Discuss any threatened or pending litigation or disciplinary action the company or principals may be involved in. Discuss any other legal liability or insurance problems.

Potential Risks and Problems

Describe and discuss in the same manner as above the problems and risks that may present themselves. Discuss what circumstances or situations would prompt these to happen and how you would deal with them if they did.

Worst Case Scenario

Give a "worst case" scenario of all inherent and potential risks that the company may suffer. Summarize the downside and what, if anything, could be salvaged or recovered if these risks did materialize.

Common Mistakes to Avoid

- Failure to identify market barriers

- Failure to identify uncontrollable variables

- Failure to state inability to guard trade secrets (having no patent or noncompete agreements if a key member of your team leaves to join a competitor)

- Failure to give an honest assessment of the "downside"

- Failure to mention pending litigation or other legal liability problems

LORD PUBLISHING, INC., 1988

Module 14 — Financial Data and Projections

Suggested Length   As needed

Objective   To illustrate current financial status and projections. To describe the type of financing desired; the amount; payback terms and potential return on investments

Note: Your should read through this entire module before you start answering the questions.

Pertinent Questions   1. Do you have past and/or current financial statements for the past three to five years?

_____

_____

Do you have past and/or current financial statements for the company?

_____

_____

Do you have past and/or current financial statements on yourself and other principals?

_____

_____

2. If your fiscal year ended over three months ago, do you have recent comparative interim financial statements for your company?

_____

_____

3. Do you have copies of company federal income tax returns for the last three years?

_____

_____

4. What are the financial projections for this venture for the first three to five years? (Should be included as an exhibit in your business plan).
   by month for the first year
   by quarter for the second and third year
   annually after the third year

   _____

   _____

5. Are these projections based on debt or equity financing?

   _____

   _____

   _____

6. How do these projections compare with industry norms? (Are the costs, revenues, profits, etc. higher or lower than similar businesses?)

   _____

   _____

   _____

7. What assumptions are the projections based on?
   give explanations
   give best-case, worst-case scenarios

   _____

   _____

   _____

   _____

8. What are the venture's start-up and research and development costs? (provide itemized list)

   _____

   _____

   _____

9. What are the costs to produce the product and get it into the market?

   _____

   _____

   _____

10. What are the venture's most significant costs?

    _____

    _____

    How volatile are they?

    _____

    _____

    How do you plan to minimize them?

    _____

    _____

11. Do you have a cost and cash flow control system in place? (your procedures for monitoring and authorizing expenses)

    _____

    _____

12. If your venture is a going concern, what are your accounts receivable?

    _____

    _____

    Have you made provisions for writing off bad debts?

    _____

    _____

13. Have you measured every phase of the venture's operation in terms of profit and loss? (Every department, piece of equipment, employee should be viewed as a profit center.)

    _____

    _____

14. What are the margins? (difference between the cost to produce your product(s) and expected sales projections)?

    _____

    _____

    Does the projected sales volume justify entering the market?

    _____

    _____

    _____

15. Have you done an analysis of your capitalization decisions?
    lease/purchase
    tax consequences
    cash flow consequences

    _____

    _____

16. Have you done an analysis of your fixed costs versus variable
    costs?

    _____

    _____

    _____

17. Have you done an analysis of cost alternatives?
    subcontracting possibilities
    shared services
    in-house vs. out-of-house expenses

    _____

    _____

    _____

18. Have you done a break-even analysis?

    _____

    _____

19. Have you forecasted the amount of product you will have to
    inventory?

    _____

    _____

    _____

20. How much money do you need? How will it be used?
    investment capital (property, equipment, etc.)
    working capital (operating, inventory,etc.)

    _____

    _____

    _____

21. What will be the effect on the business with the injection of new
    funds?

    _____

    _____

    _____

22. Will the money be required all at once, or injected over a period of time?

_____

_____

_____

23. Will these funds be raised from debt, equity or both?

_____

_____

_____

24. What collateral is being offered?

_____

_____

_____

25. Will this be the first request for outside funding?

_____

_____

_____

If not, who else has invested?

_____

_____

26. Who has/will be approached for investment?
results
committed

_____

_____

_____

27. How much have you and other principals invested?
percent ownership?

_____

_____

_____

What is the rationale for the proposed share distribution?

_____

_____

_____

28. What access to funding sources do you have that you may qualify for? (Check and describe)
    ☐ state bonds
    ☐ government land grants
    ☐ SBA (Small Business Administration) programs
    ☐ SBIR (Small Business Innovation Research) programs
    ☐ other _____

    _____

    _____

    _____

29. What are the terms of investment?
    price per share or partnership unit
    minimum amount

    _____

    _____

    _____

30. What may be the dilution of percentage of ownership of the initial investors?

    _____

    _____

    _____

31. What provisions are made for investor liquidity?

    _____

    _____

    _____

32. What is the payback period?

    _____

    _____

    _____

33. What is the potential return to investors?

    _____

    _____

    _____

How does this compare to what investors are earning from competitors and the industry in general?

_____

_____

_____

34. If there will be any ownership authorized, but not issued what percent? _____

   intended use _____

_____

_____

_____

35. Do you eventually plan to go public? When?

_____

_____

_____

Do you plan to eventually sell the company to a large corporation? When?

_____

_____

_____

36. Are the end results of financing in line (harmony) with the company's stated objectives?

_____

_____

_____

Does it allow for better control and flexibility?

_____

_____

_____

Does it provide for needed resources?

_____

_____

_____

37. Have your finances and projections been reviewed by an accountant?

_____

_____

_____

38. What leases, loan agreements or contracts are currently with the venture?

_____

_____

_____

Subheadings to Include

Funding Request/Terms of Investment
Current Financial Statements
Proformas
Assumptions

What to Accomplish

This section is highly scrutinized by potential investors. Most sophisticated investors will undertake an independent financial analysis of the venture. It must be thorough and convincing. Document the need for funds. Demonstrate that you will use them responsibly and how they will ensure your success. Use a standard format in the preparation of all statements. Show that your projections are realistic, based on the margins between your cost to operate and expected sales. Back these projections up with reasonable assumptions.

The following is a suggested sequence of presentation:

Funding Request

State the amount and type (debt or equity) of funding being sought. Describe the intended use of the funds. Give a breakdown of how the money will be applied, i.e., capital equipment, property, facilities, inventory and operating costs. Discuss what effect the capital will have on the business in terms of growth and profitability.

State when the money will be needed. Include a graph showing the amount and timing of the funds. Discuss the level of investment already made in the venture. State whether it is funded internally or from outside sources. Discuss the amount of stock or ownership that will be made available, but not issued in the current offering. Discuss future funding expectations and the stages it will be needed. Describe how the unissued ownership may be used at future stages and how, if at all, this future fundraising will effect the current offering.

Describe the terms of investment. State the minimum amount to participate. Describe how this offering will dilute the ownership of the initial and subsequent investors. Discuss the rationale for the proposed distribution. Discuss the payback period and potential return on investment. Describe why the investment is attractive and how it compares to other deals within the industry. Discuss any provisions for investor liquidity and the earliest date the investor can recover initial investment.

State any collateral being offered. Discuss who you have already approached about investing and the results of the contact. Discuss any access you have to additional investors or funding sources. Discuss what the total exposure of the investor is if the deal goes bad. What percent, if any, of the investment could be recouped via tax benefits, liquidation, or other means.

Finally, describe how this package fits in with the venture objectives and why the ownership structure being proposed is the most suitable for the business.

Current Financial Statements

If the venture is already in operation, you will need to provide three basic statements:

1. profit and loss sheet

2. cash flow sheet

3. balance sheet

Although it is wise to have complete itemized statements available for the purposes of reviewing a business plan, the reader will be largely interested in the bottom line. For this reason, a condensed statement with all three sheets on one page will suffice. A sample can be found in this guide's Appendix. It may also be necessary for you to have past tax returns on hand.

Another helpful tool to include is a budget deviation analysis. This simply shows the difference between your budgeted expenses and expected sales, and the actual outcome. Not only is it an excellent internal tool for management, it also shows potential investors that you gauge expectations against actual developments. Be sure to explain unusual fluctuations. A sample form can be found in this guide's Appendix.

Describe the terms of any existing leases, loan agreements, or contracts currently binding the company.

Proformas

Your projections should be based on realistic expectations. Be ready to justify all profits or losses for a 3–5 year period. You should provide proformas for the following:

1. Projected income (P&L) statement
2. Projected cash flow statement
3. Projected balance statement

These statements should reflect the effect of the proposed financing on a monthly basis for the first year, on a quarterly basis for the second and third year, and on an annual basis thereafter. It is also helpful to present these statements in three ways: upside, downside, and probable. Prospective investors also like to see long-range thinking, which implies you plan to be involved and committed to the venture for many years. Probable projections for 3–5 years are sufficient to carry this section. Include all other statements in your appendix.

It is also to your benefit to provide a break-even analysis and estimated costs and budgets for each department; i.e., marketing, manufacturing, inventory, administrative overhead, etc.

A sample of some of these statements are included in this guide's Appendix.

When reviewing your projections, the reader will be sizing up the potential to make a healthy return on the required investment. But invariably, the reader will be thinking, "What is the worst that could happen?" You should be prepared to discuss the alternatives if the downside is realized.

Assumptions

Assumptions are a natural part of predicting the future, especially when it applies to economics, markets, and financial projections. Your projections are only as good as the assumptions under which the projections are based. The trick is in making reasonable assumptions that those concerned with the startup feel are valid. Use this section of your business plan to state the assumptions you are making. Discuss why you feel they are valid and what alternatives you may pursue if they do not materialize.

Listed below are some considerations you may have to address when discussing what you are basing your assumptions on:

- Inventory turnover
- Accounts receivable collection period (and bad debt projections)
- Accounts payable payment period
- Purchasing in volume

- Extent of startup and future capital expenditures

- Useful life of company's assets and related depreciation schedules

- Interest rates on debt

- Effective income tax rate

- Expected capacity and utilization of plant and equipment; availability of suppliers and components

- Variable levels of production based on downtime, holidays, number of shifts and employees, percentage of overtime, etc. (How are you arriving at your maximum output?)

- Sales and share of the market based on characteristics of market, penetration strategies, pricing, competition, and trends of the industry

- Growth and success based on management training and learning curve
    - addition of specialized personnel
    - salaries, commissions, profits sharing levels

- Sales by markets and products. Margins of each.

Proformas Using Microcomputers

To help you prepare financial projections, we recommend the use of a software package called *Ronstadt's FINANCIALS*. FINANCIALS was designed and developed by entrepreneurs for other entrepreneurs who are neither financial nor computer experts. Since assumptions drive the venture creation process, you only need to enter the values for some underlying assumptions about the venture to generate a complete set of financial projections (using an IBM or compatible microcomputer). These include a sales forecast, income statement, balance sheet, and cash flow statement.

The program comes with six industry and two general models: Contract Services, Manufacturing, Retail, Professional Services, Real Estate, Wholesale Distribution, General Purpose, and Standard — and a Personal Finance Model (because your venture's financial status and your personal financial condition are intertwined). Appendix B provides a brief overview of the software and each of the industry models.

All you need to do is follow the steps below:

1. Select the industry model from Appendix B representing the industry in which your venture will be operating.

2. Make copies of the Assumption Statement for that industry, one for each scenario.

3. Gather the needed information for the scenario under consideration and complete the Assumption Statement using *Ronstadt's FINANCIALS*.

4. Print out the projected financial statements.

5. Repeat Steps 3 and 4 for any other scenarios under consideration.

If you do not have access to a microcomputer and *Ronstadt's FINANCIALS*, you will have to prepare your financial projections using more traditional methods, as follows:

1. Select the industry model from Appendix B representing the industry in which your venture will be operating.

2. Make copies of the Assumption Statement for that industry, one for each scenario.

3. Gather the needed information for the scenario as shown on the Assumption Statement.

4. Follow the steps in the Appendix for manual completion of the projected Profit & Loss Statement, Balance Sheet, and Cash Flow.

5. Repeat Steps 3 and 4 for other scenarios under consideration.

Using the information contained in the sets of financial projections (prepared from *Ronstadt's FINANCIALS* or manually), you are now able to answer the key financial resource questions.

1. How much money do you need to start or expand your venture?

2. When will you need this money?

3. Should the money be debt or equity?

4. Where should you get this money?

5. What is the value of this money to you in terms of the equity you will likely give up for it?

For a comprehensive discussion of the important issues in financing a new or existing business, we recommend Ronstadt, *Entreprenurial Finance: Taking Control of Your Financial Decision Making,* Lord Publishing, Inc., Natick, MA, 1988.

Common Mistakes to Avoid

- Faillure to provide a cash flow analysis and other financial statements

- Unrealistic sales and profit projections

- Failure to make reasonable assumptions (or showing what you are basing your projections on)

- Underestimating operating expenses, taxes, and other "hidden" costs

- Terms of the deal are not clear; minimum investment, return on investment, payback period, etc.

- The venture is too high a risk considering potential return being offered

- Salaries, office furnishings, and other "fringes" are out of line (too high) for the startup

- Failure to show that the founders (and other key people involved have made a reasonable financial commitment (put their own money on the line)

- Amount of stock, or other return on investment being offered, is not in line with the proposed investment (giving up too little in proportion to what you are asking them to contribute)

- Failure to explain why the ownership structure and terms of the deal are in the best interest of all concerned

- The proposed return on investment is not in line (too little) with what investors are earning from similar ventures

- No provisions made for transfer of investment or liquidity if the investors want out (or the company wants them out)

- Failure to demonstrate the tax benefits of the investment

- Failure to project the downside if sales don't go as expected

- Failure to have your financial statements and projections prepared and/or checked by a reputable accountant (you can bet the investor will)

LORD PUBLISHING, INC., 1988

The Finishing Touches

The Big Test

Does your plan accomplish the following?:

1. Makes it clear what business you are in.

2. Demonstrates that you are solving a problem or filling a customer opportunity in a unique and special way.

3. Clearly identifies success determinants.

   - sales margin
   - advertising/promotion
   - price
   - cost control/efficiency

4. Identifies major strengths and advantages.

   - credit availability
   - equipment/plant
   - management/personnel
   - existing contracts
   - letter of intent
   - limited competition

5. Identifies major weaknesses.

   - location
   - competition
   - suppliers
   - unskilled labor
   - undercapitalized
   - poor market identity

6. Shows that the venture has checks and balances between finance, manufacturing/operations, marketing, management and other areas of expertise.

7. Demonstrates that the timing is right.

   - economical forces
   - financing/interest rates
   - market forces

LORD PUBLISHING, INC., 1988

8. Outlines your objectives and time frames, how you will get there.

9. Outlines the inherent problems and potential risks involved.

10. Clearly states what you will do with the money invested.

11. Discusses what the terms of the deal are, potential return on investment over a specified period, and reasonable assumptions on which the projections are based.

12. Summarizes how you will update, revise and refine the plan as situations and events unfold.

The Investor Test

Are you prepared to address five proverbial question asked of new ventures by prospective investors?

1. If this is such a great idea, how come no one else is doing it?

   This question is designed to put you on the spot. The investor may be skeptical because if no one else has tried this, or a similar venture before, it may be because there is no money to be made in it. Your answer may very well be, "There will be competitors emerging after we pave the way and create a sizable market." They want you to justify why it is a viable opportunity.

2. Why are you in this venture?

   This question is designed to find out what motivates you. Some people want independence, others are more motivated by sheer profit. There are always more reasons to shy away from a deal than there are to risk investing in it. For this reason, investors want to know what you think you will get out of it and what makes you think you can do it. Service to humanity is good and well, but investors want to be assured that you have the confidence and burning desire to be successful. They want to know that you are in business to earn a profit.

3. Have you talked to others in the same, or similar business?

   This question is designed to find out how much you know about the industry. Investors want to see that you have done your homework, that you have a good handle on most of the operation's variables, i.e., suppliers, transportation, location, labor, insurance, etc., and that you learn from others in the business.

4. Have you tried the product out in the market?

   This question is designed to find out if you are market conscious. Investors want to know people will buy the product and that you can adapt to their changing needs.

5. Has your plan been critiqued by an accountant, lawyer, banker, management consultant and/or other professionals?

This question is designed to find out if this is a one man show, or if you are a team player. Investors want to see that you can access resources and harness expertise. They want to see that all the appropriate disciplines are actively involved, which minimizes their risk.

The Final Test: Do you and your plan have M.O.R.E.?

Motive — Are you and your team motivated? Do you have the drive and ambition to be successful?

Opportunity — Does an identifiable opportunity exist? Is the opportunity big enough and attractive enough to pursue?

Resource — Are the resources needed for success available, and how will you use these resources if they are made available?

Experience — Have you been in this business before? Do you know it inside and out? Have you recruited experienced people to manage and run the important operations?

Packaging Your Business Plan

Your plan should be typewritten, single spaced. The headings and subheadings should be clearly distinguishable and easy to access. Use standard elite, nonscript type (except to emphasize significant points). Have a person who writes well check it for spelling, punctuation and grammar.

Have your lawyer, accountant and other professionals review the plan. Have them sign-off on the sections they helped prepare (as an example, your accountant may include his name and company at the bottom of the financial section). You should number each plan and have a place for the signature of those to whom you are circulating the plan. This conveys the value of the plan and helps protect its proprietary nature. If appropriate, include a private placement disclaimer as the first sheet. It is also a good idea to include a personalized foreword to each person to whom you circulate the plan, highlighting their particular interests.

Finally, you will want your plan to make a good first impression. The cover should have a rich feel and look, but not be ostentatious or overly expensive. You don't want to give the impression that you squander money. The name of your company or project should be printed on the cover.

Appendices

Appendix A:
Supporting Documentation

Appendix B:
Financial Projections

Appendix A: Supporting Documentation

Suggested Length   As needed

Objective   To provide more comprehensive documentation that supports the
                         information and claims made in various sections of the business plan

Pertinent Questions 1. Do you have any professional photos of the product, facilities or
                             equipment?

                             _____

                             _____

                         2. What contracts have you signed? (Check and describe)

                             ☐ management, employment, nondisclosure/non-competition

                             ☐ suppliers, leases

                             ☐ customers, investors

                             ☐ professional counsel

                             ☐ other _____

                             _____

                             _____

                         3. Do you hold patent, trade, service mark or copyright protection
                             papers?

                             _____

                             _____

                         4. Have you developed a biography of all self-performed or
                             professional research, studies or surveys conducted in
                             conjunction with this venture?

                             _____

                             _____

                         5. Have you charted the venture's sales, profits and break-even
                             point by product/service and markets?

                             _____

                             _____

6. Do you have a chart that names your major competitors, with their share of the market and annual sales over a 3–5 year period?

   _____

   _____

7. Have you done a competitive comparison chart of your venture's strengths and weaknesses?

   _____

   _____

8. Have you any samples of your advertising materials?

   _____

   _____

9. Do you have resumes and personal references from customers, suppliers, bankers, former employers, etc., on each of the principals?

   _____

   _____

10. Do you have personal financial statements for each of the principals?

   _____

   _____

11. Do you have job descriptions for major positions and support personnel?

   _____

   _____

12. Do you have an organizational chart illustrating the lines of authority and responsibility?

   _____

   _____

13. Have you outlined your management control systems?

   _____

   _____

14. Do you have a timeline chart depicting significant milestones and their priority for completion?

   _____

   _____

15. Have you listed your equipment and other capital expenditures, with a description and the cost of each?

   _____

   _____

16. Have you graphed the amount of money and timing of the funds to be infused?

   _____

   _____

17. Have you done a budget deviation analysis?

   _____

   _____

18. Have you current and projected statements of:
   profit and loss
   cash flow
   balance sheets

   _____

   _____

19. Have you developed a budget for each department or profit center?

   _____

   _____

Subheadings to Include

The following is a list of exhibits that you might include in your Appendix:

A. Company and Product(s)/Services Support Materials

   1. Photos of the product, equipment, facilities

   2. Patents, trademarks, service marks, or copyright documents

   3. Bibliography of research, testing, and studies conducted

B. Legal Support Materials

   1. Partnership agreements or management contracts

   2. Agent/rep agreements or employment contracts

   3. Noncompetition/nondisclosure agreements

   4. Equipment, facilities, leases, and supplier agreements

C. Market Support Materials

1. Magazine, newspaper, trade journal articles

2. Marketing, advertising brochures, drawings, mailings, and materials

3. Market share and sales chart, 3–5 years

4. Competitive comparison of strengths and weaknesses

5. Customers contacted and status (signed orders)

6. Letters of intent

D. Management/Ownership Support Materials

1. Resumes of key people, references, and letter of recommendation

2. Management control systems outline

3. Significant milestones and timeframes

E. Administrative and Personnel Support Materials

1. Organizational chart

2. Staff training outline for each department/function

3. Job descriptions of key positions

4. Bookkeeping, purchasing, inventory, and other control systems

F. Financial/Investment Support Materials (See Appendix B)

1. Break-even analysis of company by product, markets, and total operations

2. Financial statements of company and owners

3. Equipment and capital expenditures listing

4. Graph of amount of funds and timing for investment

5. Budget deviation analysis on operations, previous year

6. Budgets for each department or profit center

7. Additional profit and loss, cash flow and balance statements showing upside, downside, or extended projections

What to Accomplish   Demonstrate you have done a significant amount of thinking and work in all areas of the venture. Your exhibits will lend credibility to your plan. More importantly, they allow the reader to visualize your accomplishments and goals. Make sure they are attractive, readable, and understandable.

The sequence and format of presentation should be similar to the one above, under "Subheadings to Include."

Common Mistakes to Avoid

- Exhibits poorly reproduced, difficult to read

- Too technical, or explanations of how to read and interpret the information not provided (some graphs and charts require a legend)

- Failure to list the source or stating on what the information is based

- Arranging material poorly throughout the business plan (most documentation should be used as exhibits and placed in back as reference)

Sample Organizational Chart

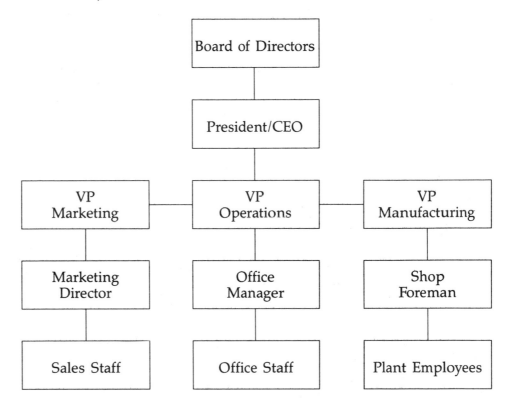

**Sample Operations
Layout Chart**

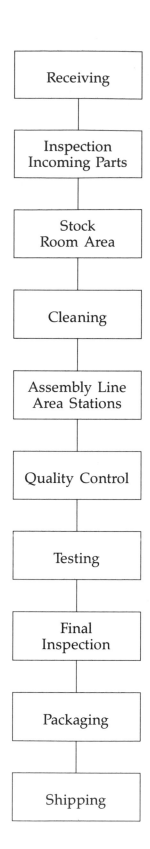

Sample Time Line Chart

Date	Milestones	Assignment	Alternative Action
1/25/89	Mock-up model completed	Thompson	Drawing
2/28/89	Schematics drafted	Thompson	Outline of specs.
3/1/89	Working prototype	Thompson/Jones	Subcontract to University
5/1/89	Evaluation/testing of prototype completed	Thompson/Jones	Make necessary revisions
	Secure additional seed capital needed	Hendricks	Go Ahead Scrap project
6/1/89	Install customer test site	Thompson	License to existing manufacturer
	Assemble second unit	Jones	
6/30/89	Attend industry trade show – distribute literature – demonstrate prototype	Martin	Direct mail campaign Ad in industry
7/30/89	Complete Business Plan and Marketing Plan	Hendricks	Executive Summaries to distribute on limited basis
9/1/89	Determine venture goals	Full Team	Seek Financing Full Production Sell Project License Product

Appendix B: Financial Projections

- ■ RONSTADT'S FINANCIALS

- ■ ASSUMPTION STATEMENTS FOR

    - RETAIL STORES

    - PROFESSIONAL SERVICES

    - CONTRACT SERVICES

    - MANUFACTURING VENTURES

    - REAL ESTATE VENTURES

    - WHOLESALE DISTRIBUTORS

    - GENERAL PURPOSE PROJECTIONS

    - PERSONAL FINANCE

- ■ PREPARING FINANCIAL PROJECTIONS MANUALLY

LORD PUBLISHING, INC., 1988

Ronstadt's FINANCIALS

What Is It?

Ronstadt's FINANCIALS is a software package that allows non-financial and non-computer experts to rapidly generate financial projections (proformas) for their ventures and/or their personal use. The software embodies state-of-the-art financial, accounting, and entrepreneurship expertise which gives decision makers the opportunity to produce financial scenarios that contain projected Sales Forecasts, Income Statements, Balance Sheets, Cash Flows, Financial Ratios, Break Evens, and supporting budgets. The program ties all these projections together. You need only alter your basic assumptions to view the changes in all these projections.

Financial projections are the heart of financial strategies. Unfortunately, decision makers have been forced to relinquish control over the development of financial projections to specialists, who frequently do not fully understand the decision makers venture. Many decision makers do not have the time nor capability to develop their own financial projections. Consequently, the task has often been left undone or given to an accountant or other specialist who rarely has the strategic perspective of an owner/manager.

Too often the end result is the development of a financial strategy that handicaps an enterprise...a financial strategy that the decision maker has not internalized because he or she did not participate in the development of its core. This process is one where strategic options are explored, where basic assumptions are altered, and where the financial implications of these changing assumptions are projected into the future to see their likely consequences. It is not a process that should be delegated lightly to another.

In an age where insufficient financial resources are often the reason for, if not the cause of, venture failure, Ronstadt's FINANCIALS offers an opportunity to place control of financial decision making squarely in the hands of the leaders charged with starting or expanding a venture. We've worked hard to make Ronstadt's FINANCIALS a practical tool — one that's powerful yet easy to use, a software program that will truly help you to realize your goals and dreams.

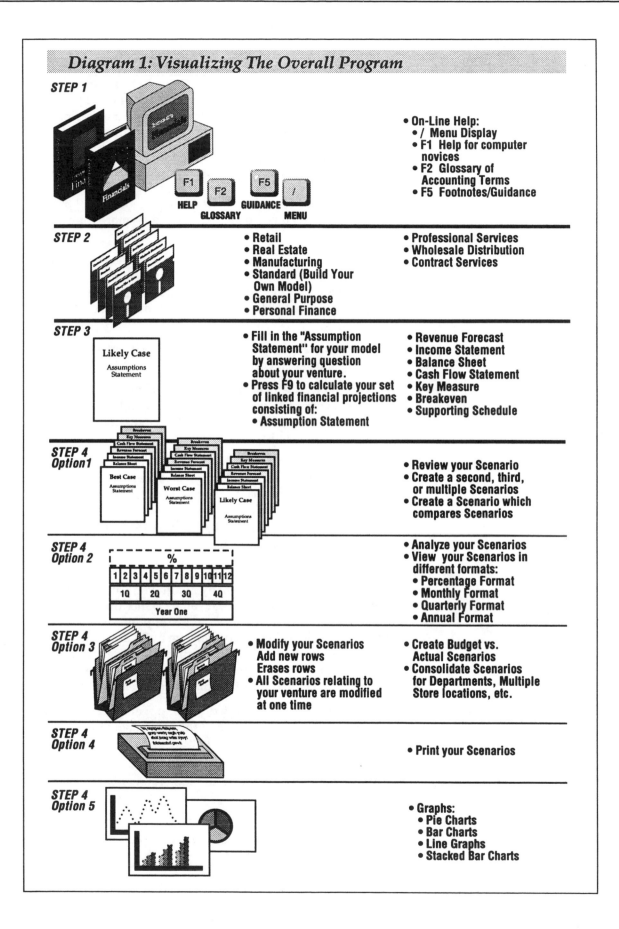

Diagram 1: Visualizing The Overall Program

STEP 1

- On-Line Help:
  - / Menu Display
  - F1 Help for computer novices
  - F2 Glossary of Accounting Terms
  - F5 Footnotes/Guidance

F1 — HELP
F2 — GLOSSARY
F5 — GUIDANCE
/ — MENU

STEP 2

- Retail
- Real Estate
- Manufacturing
- Standard (Build Your Own Model)
- General Purpose
- Personal Finance
- Professional Services
- Wholesale Distribution
- Contract Services

STEP 3

Likely Case
Assumptions Statement

- Fill in the "Assumption Statement" for your model by answering question about your venture.
- Press F9 to calculate your set of linked financial projections consisting of:
  - Assumption Statement
- Revenue Forecast
- Income Statement
- Balance Sheet
- Cash Flow Statement
- Key Measure
- Breakeven
- Supporting Schedule

STEP 4 Option 1

Best Case / Worst Case / Likely Case
Assumptions Statement

- Review your Scenario
- Create a second, third, or multiple Scenarios
- Create a Scenario which compares Scenarios

STEP 4 Option 2

%
1 2 3 4 5 6 7 8 9 10 11 12
1Q 2Q 3Q 4Q
Year One

- Analyze your Scenarios
- View your Scenarios in different formats:
  - Percentage Format
  - Monthly Format
  - Quarterly Format
  - Annual Format

STEP 4 Option 3

- Modify your Scenarios
  Add new rows
  Erases rows
- All Scenarios relating to your venture are modified at one time
- Create Budget vs. Actual Scenarios
- Consolidate Scenarios for Departments, Multiple Store locations, etc.

STEP 4 Option 4

- Print your Scenarios

STEP 4 Option 5

- Graphs:
  - Pie Charts
  - Bar Charts
  - Line Graphs
  - Stacked Bar Charts

Library Files

An important element incorporated in Ronstadt's FINANCIALS are the eight industry models that have been developed for you. These models address the majority of entrepreneurial business ventures and have distinct assumption data and unique features.

The Library Files are designed to be used in their current form, or as a nucleus for developing your business specific set of financial statements. We feel that by reviewing the various design approaches taken and formulas provided, these models will prove extremely beneficial if you plan to create larger, more complex models.

All the Library Files request similar assumption data pertaining to the Balance Sheet and Cash Flow Analysis needed to create your own financial statements. This common data, together with industry specific assumption data, is found in the Assumption Statement.

All assumption data for your models are to be inserted only in the Assumption Statement.

The Assumption Statement is divided into five sections: Revenue, Expenses, Balance Sheet, Cash Flow and Breakeven. Since the Revenue and Expense sections are industry specific, they will be covered later in this section.

The Balance Sheet section may have questions regarding material (product) purchases. You will be asked for the number of months needed to purchase material (goods). Based on the number of months entered, the model will enter that future period's cost of goods as a purchase in the current period.

The Cash Flow section has information relating to cash collections and payments.

You will be asked for the percent by month you anticipate collecting your opening accounts receivable balance (base period), if applicable. It also asks you for your assumptions on your current revenues/sales collection percentage by 30-day time periods. All of the models will automatically calculate your collections and spread the amounts in the Cash Flow Analysis by the percentages entered in the Assumption Statement.

The same information is requested for the opening accounts payable (base period), if applicable, and the percentages by 30-day time periods you project your current expenses to be paid within.

A similar spreading of the expenses paid is shown in the Cash Flow Analysis.

Fixed Assets Purchased

Allows you to enter amounts for specific property and equipment projected to be purchased by month.

© *LORD PUBLISHING, INC., 1988*

Long Term Debt

If you currently have a loan outstanding or plan to incur any debt during the year, this section allows you to insert the number of months the loan will be repaid in, and your annual interest rate charged.

Line of Credit

If you have a bank line of credit established, you may enter the annual interest rate and the maximum borrowing availalbe on the line.

Minimum Cash Balance

Certain banking covenants may require you to maintain a minimum cash balance (compensating balance) or you may not want your cash balance to dip below a minimum amount based on your personal comfort level.

Additional Funding

If you plan to finance any equipment, create a notes payable, or add new equity that may be required as working capital to fund your existing operation, the Cash Flow Analysis will ask you to insert these amounts in this section of the Assumption Statement.

After you have entered your projections in the Assumption Statement, your Revenue Forecast, Income Statement, Balance Sheet, Projected Breakeven, Cash Flow Analysis, and Key Measures are instantly and automatically created.

||||||||||||||| **NOTE**

If you have an existing business, you may enter your opening balances for your Balance Sheet (Base Period). On a new venture, this section would be left with zero balances. Also, if any expenses or questions asked are not applicable to your business, you may leave them with zero balances. However, your opening (Base Period) Balance Sheet must balance.

Cash Flow

The Cash Flow being such a critical statement, has been developed to take into account information entered regarding your Line of Credit.

The Cash Flow analyzes your cash inflows and outflows, and will automatically, based upon the Cash Balance Before Funding and the Minimum Cash Balance required, calculate whether you have enough cash to pay down any existing line of credit outstanding, or the need to borrow against your line of credit up to the maximum allowed. It will also prompt you if you have enough or need additional funds, based on your minimum cash requirements.

Although the models will automatically "toggle" between borrowing or paying down the line of credit, you still have the flexibility to either increase long-term debt payable or add new equity in the business at any time. This will adjust the amount needed to borrow or pay down on the line of credit.

The Revenue and Expense section of the Assumption Statement are industry specific and therefore a brief explanation of certain areas in the Assumptions Statement for each of the models are included.

Retail

A business that sells products to consumers from storefront locations, i.e., clothing, liquor, hardware, gift shop.

Revenues

We have developed this model having a three-store locations. The individual annual store sales can be inserted. If you plan to have one store, just leave Stores B and C with zero sales. Since your sales are usually seasonal, you have the ability to enter a percentage of sales for each of the twelve months. A "sum of monthly %" row has been included so you will know when a 100% of sales has been allocated. (This is a calculated amount.) The percentage growth next year is important because purchasing goods in future months is based on lead times. This will account for the increase in goods (inventory) necessary to purchase, based on monthly sales next year. The Cost of Sales row is entered as a percentage of sales by store.

Income Statement

The expenses are listed by individual stores and a corporate administrative location. The expenses are either entered as monthly dollar amounts or a percentage of monthly sales depending on the type of expense. Depreciation of fixed assets is based on the number of years (useful life) and calculated on a straight-line basis.

Professional Service

A business that provides services on a time fee basis, i.e., legal, accounting, consulting, advertising, etc.

Revenues

This section in the Assumption Statement is divided into Partners, Associates, and Staff billings. It has a row for number of partners, the billing rate, any increases in the billing rate during the year, total available hours for each partner per month, and the percentage of the total available hours that are billable. The same information is asked for Associates and Staff. Also, there is a row for the percentage of monthly billings that will be absorbed (reduction of fees), and what percentage of the hours available for billing will actually be invoiced each month. (An assumption is made that whatever does not get billed in one month will be billed the following month.)

Income Statement

This section is separated between client related expenses and operating expenses. The client expense has a row for the monthly percentage that is recoverable (What % of the total expenses incurred do you feel you can bill?) as well as what percentage of the monthly expenses incurred will be billed in the current month. (An assumption is also made that whatever does not get billed in one month will be billed the next month.)

Operating expenses are shown as either percentages or dollar amounts, depending on the type of expense.

Corporate Insurance

We have taken into account the fact that annual insurance premiums are paid at one time but expensed during the term of the policy. We therefore have a section which asks for the month in which the premium is paid. If you have entered in the Base Period on the Balance Sheet, any prepaid insurance, the next section asks you how many months are remaining to expense for this amount.

Contract Service

A business that provides services on a flat rate fee per contract or subscription based, i.e., cleaning, driving, school, answering service, gardening, etc.)

Revenues

We developed this model based on the number of jobs per month and the average revenues realized per job. Cost of Sales is based upon the percentage of revenues that applies to materials used on the job and the outside (subcontracted) labor needed for the job or an actual dollar amount per month for materials and outside labor.

Income Statement

Common monthly operating expenses are listed and the assumptions are either in percentages or dollar amounts.

Manufacturing

A business building/producing products on a per unit basis, i.e., computer, furniture, luggage, etc.

Revenues

This model assumes two products, A and B, are manufactured for sale. The projected sales in units are entered into the Assumption Statement. The selling price per unit is requested for each product.

Production Schedule per product - based upon your sales forecast, you may enter in the amount of units that you plan to manufacture. Producing more units than your sales forecast requires will create an increase in finished goods inventory. You also need to enter the percentage growth next year for material purchase calculations. Since this model was developed using standard cost, you may enter in the standard labor and overhead, and material cost for each product.

Income Statement

As with the other models, monthly expenses are entered as constants each month or as fluctuating amounts for each month during the year (i.e., Advertising). Depreciation is based on useful life in years for the type of asset, and is calculated at straight line.

In addition, the Balance Sheet will have inventories broken out by Finished Goods and Raw Material which is unique to this model.

Real Estate

A business involved in real estate management or rental property, i.e., landlord, real estate investment, etc.

Revenues

We developed this section to account for both commercial property which leases space based on square footage and on annual dollar amount per square foot, and residential property which is based upon the number of units and the monthly rent per apartment. We have added rows for percentage increases in the annual square footage and monthly rents, and percentage of vacancy.

Income Statement

We have designed this section based upon commonly used expenses incurred in property management.

Casualty Insurance

We have taken into account the fact that annual insurance premiums are paid at one time but expensed over the term of the policy. We therefore have a section which asks the month in which the premium is paid. If you have entered in the Base Period on the Balance Sheet any prepaid insurance, the next section asks you how many months are remaining to expense this amount.

Real Estate Taxes

This section is unique to this model. Since property taxes are a major expense and can have a material cash flow impact based on when they are paid, we developed this section as follows: First we ask you what the annual real estate taxes are. Then we need to know if they are collected monthly by a lending institution or paid directly by you. If you enter 1, the model will take the annual taxes and allocate them over twelve months in the Cash Flow. If you answer 0, you need to enter the month of the first tax payment and the number of months between payments. (i.e., if taxes are paid twice a year, your answer to the number of months between payments is 6.) The Cash Flow will accurately reflect the payment of these taxes.

Wholesale Distribution

A business that purchases goods for sale to resellers (middle marketeers), i.e., food, tires, sporting goods, etc.

Revenues

This model is set up using one product line with two products within the product line. The questions asked in the Assumption Statement are:

Annual sales by product

The returns percentage you may have

The monthly allocation of the annual sales

What's the average Cost of Sales percentage

As we have seen in some of the other models involving inventories, we have provided rows asking for the percentage growth and the lead time necessary for purchasing products.

Income Statements

The assumptions are broken out to accommodate both field and inside salespeople, and warehouse employees on salary and on an hourly basis, as well as usual expenses incurred in a distribution operation.

General Purpose

This model was developed for quick projections or feasibility studies aimed at any type of business by answering only a few basic assumptions.

This model is unique from all the other models in that the assumptions asked are based on an "annual" basis. The model was derived from the Contract Service model and most of the questions asked are from that model. The formulas, however, are directly related to the time period (M, Q, Y) you establish in the scenario setting. If, at any time during the session you want to change the time period, the statement will automatically be readjusted without changing assumption data.

Standard

This model contains ONLY the standard rows. It is for a company that has a specific or unique business in mind. Although the models above may be modified to fit a specific need, using the Standard model may be faster for those who wish to create their custom model.

Assumption Statement

Retail Stores

	Data Input
Revenue Forecast Assumptions:	
Annual Sales, Store A	$_____
Annual Sales, Store B	$_____
Annual Sales, Store C	$_____
Percent Of Sales Allocated Per Month	_____%
Sum of "Percent of Sales Allocated" Row	_____%
Growth Rate Next Year:	
Growth rate store A	_____%
Growth rate store B	_____%
Growth rate store C	_____%
Income Statement Assumptions:	
Cost of Goods: (as a percent of sales)	
Store A	_____%
Store B	_____%
Store C	_____%
Store A: Monthly Operating Expenses	
Store A manager's salary	$_____
Salespeople salaries:	
Base salaries	$_____
Commission rate	_____%
Advertising and promotion, store A	_____%
Rent, store A	$_____
Supplies, store A	_____%
Telephone, utilities, insurance, A	$_____
Store B: Monthly Operating Expenses	
Store B manager's salary	$_____
Salespeople salaries:	
Base salary	$_____
Sales commission rate	_____%
Advertising and promotion, store B	_____%
Rent, store B	$_____
Supplies, store B	_____%
Telephone, utilities, insurance, B	$_____
Store C: Monthly Operating Espense	
Store C manager's salary	$_____
Salespeople salaries:	
Salary base	$_____
Commission percentage rate	_____%
Advertising and promotion, store C	_____%
Rent, store C	$_____
Supplies, store C	_____%
Telephone, utilities, insurance, C	$_____
Store Payroll Tax And Benefit Rate	_____%
Monthly Corporate Operating Expenses:	
Monthly administrative salaries:	
Salaries, officers	$_____
Salaries, administrative	$_____
Office payroll tax and benefit rate	_____%
Monthly office expenses:	
Franchise fee	_____%
Freight and postage	$_____
Office supplies	$_____

Professional fees . . . . $_____
Rent and occupancy . . . . $_____
Telephone . . . . $_____
Travel . . . . $_____

Balance Sheet Assumptions:
    Inventory Purchases:
        Enter the lead-time in months. Necessary to purchase inventory . . . . _____
    If you entered a lead-time for purchases review your inventory on hand.
    You may need to increase or reduce purchases.
    Your adjustments may be entered below:
        Inventory adjustments store A . . . . $_____
        Inventory adjustments store B . . . . $_____
        Inventory adjustments store C . . . . $_____
    Fixed Assets Purchased:
        Fixed assets store A . . . . $_____
        Fixed assets store B . . . . $_____
        Fixed assets store C . . . . $_____
        Fixed assets corporate . . . . $_____
    Depreciation Schedule:
        Store Fixed Assets In Years . . . . $_____
        Office Fixed Assets In Years . . . . $_____

Cash Flow Assumptions:
    Prior Accounts Receivable Collected . . . . _____%
    Monthly Sales Collected:
        % Collected 0 - 30 days . . . . _____%
        % Collected 31 - 60 days . . . . _____%
        % Collected 61 - 90 days . . . . _____%
        % Collected 90+ days . . . . _____%
    Total Monthly Sales Collected . . . . _____%
    Prior Accounts Payable Paid . . . . _____%
    Monthly Expenses Paid:
        % Paid 0 - 30 days . . . . _____%
        % Paid 31 - 60 days . . . . _____%
        % Paid 61 - 90 days . . . . _____%
        % Paid 90+ days . . . . _____%
    Total Monthly Expenses Paid . . . . _____%
    Vendor Deposits Required . . . . $_____
    Line of Credit:
        Annual line of credit interest rate . . . . _____%
        Maximum line of credit . . . . $_____
    Notes Payable:
        Annual note interest rate . . . . _____%
        Term of note in months . . . . _____
    Minimum Cash Balance . . . . $_____
    Additional Funding:
        New equity . . . . $_____
        New debt (notes payable) . . . . $_____

Projected Breakeven Assumptions:
    Variable Portion Of Cost Of Goods . . . . _____%
    Variable Portion Of Store Salaries . . . . _____%
    Variable Portion Of Advertising & Promo . . . . _____%
    Variable Portion Of Corporate Salaries . . . . _____%
    Variable Portion Of Office Expenses . . . . _____%
    Variable Portion Of Professional Fees . . . . _____%
    Variable Portion Of Travel . . . . _____%

Assumption Statement

Professional Service

	Data Input
Revenue Forecast Assumptions:	
Partners Billing:	
Number of partners	_____
Partners billing rate	_____%
Increase in partners billing rate	_____%
Total available hours/partner/month	_____
Amount of hours billed per month, as	_____%
Associates Billing:	
Number of associates	_____
Associates billing rate	\$_____
Increase in associates billing rate	_____%
Total available hours per assoc/month	_____
Number of hours billed per month, as	_____%
Staff Billing:	
Number of staff	_____
Staff billing rate	\$_____
Increase in staff billing rate	_____%
Total available hours per staff/month	_____
% of available hours billed per month	_____%
Monthly Fees Absorbed Per Month, As %	_____%
Percent of Billings Invoiced Per Month	_____%
Income Statement Assumptions:	
Monthly Client Related Expenses:	
Copying and duplication	\$_____
Postage and freight	\$_____
Fax and telephone	\$_____
Travel	\$_____
Other client related expense	\$_____
Recoverable Percent of Client Expenses	_____%
Percent of Client Expenses Invoiced	_____%
Monthly Operating Expenses:	
Associates salaries	\$_____
Secretarial and administrative salaries	\$_____
Bad debt percentage per year	_____%
Dues and subscriptions	\$_____
Monthly insurance cost per member	\$_____
Corporate Insurance:	
Insurance, casualty (annual)	\$_____
Month in which your premium is paid	_____
How many months remain to expense on your opening prepaid insurance?	_____
Legal and audit	\$_____
Office expense	\$_____
Freight and postage	\$_____
Rent	\$_____
Stationery and printing	\$_____
Telephone	\$_____
Travel and entertainment	\$_____
Utilities	\$_____
Payroll tax rate:	_____%

FICA tax rate . . . .   _____%
SUTA/FUTA tax rate . . . .   _____%

Balance Sheet Assumptions:
Monthly Fixed Assets Purchased . . . . $_____
Depreciation In Years . . . .   _____

Cash Flow Assumptions:
Prior Accounts Receivable Collected . . . .   _____%
Monthly Revenues Collected:
    % Collected 0-30 days . . . .   _____%
    % Collected 31-60 days . . . .   _____%
    % Collected 61-90 days . . . .   _____%
    % Collected 90+ days . . . .   _____%

Total Monthly Revenues Collected . . . .   _____%

Prior Accounts Payable Paid . . . .   _____%
Monthly Expenses Paid:
    % Paid 0-30 days . . . .   _____%
    % Paid 31-60 days . . . .   _____%
    % Paid 61-90 days . . . .   _____%
    % Paid 90+ days . . . .   _____%

Total Monthly Expenses Paid . . . .   _____%

Vendor Deposits Required . . . . $_____
Partners' Total Monthly Draw . . . . $_____
Current Percent of Salaries Paid . . . .   _____%
Line of Credit:
    Annual line of credit interest rate . . . .   _____%
    Maximum line of credit . . . . $_____
Notes Payable:
    Annual note interest rate . . . .   _____%
    Term of note in months . . . .   _____
Minimum Cash Balance . . . . $_____
Additional Funding:
    New equity . . . . $_____
    New debt (notes payable) . . . . $_____

Projected Breakeven Assumptions:
Variable Portion of Client Related Expense . . . .   _____%
Variable Portion of Payroll Expense . . . .   _____%
Variable Portion of General Expenses . . . .   _____%
Variable Portion of Occupancy Expenses . . . .   _____%

Assumption Statement

Contract Service

Revenue Forecast Assumptions:	Data Input
Monthly Revenue:	
Average fee charged per job	$_____
Number of jobs per month	_____

Income Statement Assumptions:
Cost of Sales:
  (choose one, below):
  Material used as a percent of fee, or . . . . _____%
  Material used per job in dollars . . . . $_____
  (choose one, below):
  Contract labor used as a percent of fee, or . . . . _____%
  Contract labor used per job in dollars . . . . $_____
Monthly Salary and Wages:
  Salaries, sales . . . . $_____
  Salaries, marketing . . . . $_____
  Salaries, accounting . . . . $_____
  Salaries, administrative . . . . $_____
  Payroll tax and benefit rate . . . . _____%
  Current percent of salaries paid . . . . _____%
Monthly Occupancy Expenses:
  Rent . . . . $_____
  Insurance, casualty . . . . $_____
  Repairs and maintenance . . . . $_____
  Utilities . . . . $_____
Monthly Operating Expenses:
  Advertising and promotion . . . . $_____
  Automobile expense . . . . $_____
  Dues and subscriptions . . . . $_____
  Office expense . . . . $_____
  Permits and licenses . . . . $_____
  Professional fees . . . . $_____
  Small tools . . . . $_____
  Stationery and printing . . . . $_____
  Telephone . . . . $_____

Balance Sheet Assumptions:
Property and Equipment Purchased:
  Office equipment . . . . $_____
  Furniture and fixtures . . . . $_____
  Vehicles . . . . $_____
Depreciation Schedule:
  Office equipment (years) . . . . _____
  Furniture and fixtures (years) . . . . _____
  Vehicles (years) . . . . _____

Cash Flow Statement Assumptions:
    Prior Accounts Receivable Collected . . . . _____%
    Monthly Revenues Collected:
        % Collected 0-30 days . . . . _____%
        % Collected 31-60 days . . . . _____%
        % Collected 61-90 days . . . . _____%
        % Collected 90+ days . . . . _____%
    Total Monthly Revenues Collected . . . . _____%

    Prior Accounts Payable Paid . . . . _____%
    Monthly Expenses Paid:
        % Paid 0-30 days . . . . _____%
        % Paid 31-60 days . . . . _____%
        % Paid 61-90 days . . . . _____%
        % Paid 90+ days . . . . _____%
    Total Monthly Expenses Paid . . . . _____%

    Line of Credit:
        Annual line of credit interest rate . . . . _____%
        Maximum line of credit . . . . $_____
    Notes Payable:
        Annual note interest rate . . . . _____%
        Term of note in months . . . . _____
    Minimum Cash Balance . . . . $_____
    Additional Funding:
        New equity . . . . $_____
        New debt (Notes Payable) . . . . $_____

Projected Breakeven Assumptions:
    Variable Portion of Cost of Sales . . . . _____%
    Variable Portion of Salaries and Wages . . . . _____%
    Variable Portion of Operational Expenses . . . . _____%

Assumption Statement
Manufacturing

Revenue Forecast Assumptions:	Data Input
Unit Sales	
Sales product A	_____
Sales product B	_____
Unit Selling Price:	
Product A	$_____
Product B	$_____

Income Statement Assumptions:
Standard Cost Per Unit:

Product A (labor and overhead)	$_____
Product A (material)	$_____
Total standard cost A	$_____
Product B (labor and overhead)	$_____
Product B (material)	$_____
Total standard cost B	$_____

Operating Expenses:
Monthly salaries and wages:

Salaries, officers	$_____
Salaries, administrative	$_____
Clerical hours (monthly)	_____
Average hourly clerical rate	$_____
Payroll tax and benefit rate	_____%
Current percent of salaries paid	_____%

Monthly general office expense:

Freight and postage	$_____
Office expense	$_____
Stationery and printing	$_____
Telephone	$_____

Annual office occupancy expense:

Office square footage	_____
Rent allocation per square foot	$_____
Insurance allocation per square foot	$_____
Utility allocation per square foot.........................	$_____
Monthly advertising and promotion	$_____
Monthly travel	$_____
Monthly professional fees	$_____

Balance Sheet Assumptions:
Unit Production Schedule:

Unit production product A	_____
Product A growth rate per year	_____%
Unit production product B.................................	_____
Product B growth rate per year	_____%

Material Purchases:
Enter the lead-time in months necessary to purchase materials ...... _____
If you entered a lead-time for purchases, review your inventory on hand.

You may need to increase or reduce purchases.
    Enter any adjustments below:
        Material adjustments product A . . . . $_____
        Material adjustments product B . . . . $_____
    Fixed Assets Purchased:
        Computer equipment . . . . $_____
        Manufacturing equipment . . . . $_____
        Office equipment . . . . $_____
    Depreciation Schedule:
        Computer equipment (years) . . . . _____
        Manufacturing equipment (years) . . . . _____
        Office Equipment (years) . . . . _____

Cash Flow Statements Assumptions:
    Prior Accounts Receivable Collected . . . . _____%
    Monthly Revenues Collected:
        % Collected 0 - 30 days . . . . _____%
        % Collected 31 - 60 days . . . . _____%
        % Collected 61 - 90 days . . . . _____%
        % Collected 90+ days . . . . _____%
    Total Monthly Revenues Collected . . . . _____%

    Prior Accounts Payable Paid . . . . _____%
    Monthly Expenses Paid:
        % Paid 0 - 30 days . . . . _____%
        % Paid 31 - 60 days . . . . _____%
        % Paid 61 - 90 days . . . . _____%
        % Paid 90+ days . . . . _____%
    Total Monthly Expenses Paid . . . . _____%
    Vendor Deposits Required . . . . $_____
    Line of Credit:
        Annual line of credit interest rate . . . . _____%
        Maximum line of credit . . . . $_____
    Notes Payable:
        Annual note interest rate . . . . _____%
        Term of note in months . . . . _____
    Minimum Cash Balance . . . . $_____
    Additional Funding:
        New equity . . . . _____
        New debt (notes payable) . . . . _____

Projected Breakeven Assumptions:
    Variable Portion Of Cost Of Goods . . . . _____%
    Variable Portion Of Admin. Salary . . . . _____%
    Variable Portion Of Advertising & Promo . . . . _____%
    Variable Portion Of General Office Exp . . . . _____%
    Variable Portion Of Professional Fees . . . . _____%
    Variable Portion Of Travel . . . . _____%

Assumption Statement

Real Estate

Revenue Forecast Assumptions: <u>**Data Input**</u>

Commercial Property:

Total available square footage .... _____

Annual rent charged per square foot .... $_____

Increases in rent charged per square .... _____%

Commercial vacancy rate .... _____%

Residential Property:

Total available number of units .... _____

Average monthly rent charged per unit .... $_____

Increases in rent charged .... _____%

Residential vacancy rate .... _____%

Income Statement Assumptions:

Liability Insurance:

Insurance, casualty (annual) .... $_____

Month in which premium is paid .... _____

How many months remain to expense on
your opening prepaid insurance? .... _____

Monthly Operating Expenses:

Legal and accounting .... $_____

Office expense .... $_____

Property management fees .... _____%

Monthly repairs and maintenance:

Buildings .... $_____

Grounds .... $_____

Rubbish and snow removal .... $_____

Salaries .... $_____

Payroll tax and benefit rate .... _____%

Water and sewer .... $_____

Common utilities .... $_____

Real Estate Tax Assumptions:

Annual real estate taxes .... $_____

Are your taxes collected monthly by a lending institution?
(Enter 1 if YES, or 0 if NO) .... _____

If you answered NO, in which month(s) are
your real estate taxes due?:

Month of your first tax payment .... _____

Number of months between payments .... _____

Balance Sheet Assumptions:

Property and Equipment Purchased:

Buildings purchased .... $_____

Land purchased .... $_____

Equipment purchased .... $_____

Depreciation Schedule:

Buildings in years .... _____

Equipment in years .... _____

Cash Flow Statement Assumptions:

Prior Accounts Receivable Collected .... _____%

Percent of Rent Collected Monthly .... _____%

Prior Accounts Payable Paid .... _____%

Monthly Expenses Paid:
 % Paid 0-30 days . . . . _____%
 % Paid 31-60 days . . . . _____%
 % Paid 61-90 days . . . . _____%
 % Paid 90+ days . . . . _____%
Total Monthly Expenses Paid . . . . _____%

Line of Credit:
 Annual line of credit interest rate . . . . _____%
 Maximum line of credit . . . . $_____
Notes Payable:
 Annual note interest rate . . . . _____%
 Term of note in months . . . . _____%
Minimum Cash Balance . . . . $_____
Additional Funding:
 New equity . . . . $_____
 New debt (notes payable) . . . . $_____

Projected Breakeven Assumptions:
Variable Portion of Salaries . . . . _____%
Variable Portion of Management Fee . . . . _____%

Assumption Statement

Wholesale Distribution

Revenue Forecast Assumptions: **Data Input**

    Product Line A:

        Annual sales product 1 . . . . $_____

        Annual sales product 2 . . . . $_____

    Total Annual Return Rate . . . . _____%

    Percent Of Sales Allocated Per Month . . . . _____%

    Growth Rate Next Year . . . . _____%

Income Statement Assumptions:

    Cost of Goods: (percent of sales)

        Cost of goods product 1 . . . . _____%

        Cost of goods product 2 . . . . _____%

    Monthly Selling Expenses:

        Number of field salespeople . . . . _____

        Sales commission rate . . . . _____%

        Base salary or guaranteed draw per field salesperson . . . . $_____

        Travel expense per field salesperson . . . . $_____

        Number of telephone sales employees . . . . _____

        Salary per telephone sales employee . . . . $_____

        Advertising and promotion (% of sales) . . . . _____%

        Catalog as % of sales . . . . _____%

    Monthly Distribution Expenses:

        Distribution manager's salary . . . . $_____

        Number of warehouse employees . . . . _____

        Average hourly warehouse wage . . . . $_____

        Average number of hours/month/employee . . . . _____

        Freight-in as a percentage of purchases . . . . _____%

        Supplies as a percentage of sales . . . . _____%

    Monthly Administrative Expenses:

        Salaries and wages:

            Salaries, officers . . . . $_____

            Salaries, marketing . . . . $_____

            Salaries, accounting . . . . $_____

            Salaries, administrative . . . . $_____

            Salaries, purchasing . . . . $_____

            Payroll tax and benefit rate . . . . _____%

        Monthly Occupancy Expense:

            Rent . . . . $_____

            Insurance, casualty . . . . $_____

            Repairs and maintenance . . . . $_____

            Utilities (heat, light, water) . . . . $_____

        Monthly Other Expenses:

            Office expense . . . . $_____

            Professional fees . . . . $_____

            Telephone . . . . $_____

        Bad Debt Percent Per Year . . . . _____%

Balance Sheet Assumptions:

    Inventory Purchases:

        Enter the lead-time in months necessary to purchase inventory . . . . . _____

    If you entered a lead-time for purchases review your inventory on hand.

    You may need to increase or reduce inventory purchases.

Enter your adjustment below:

Inventory adjustments product 1 .... $_____

Inventory adjustments product 2 .... $_____

Property and Equipment Purchased:

Warehouse equipment .... $_____

Office equipment... $_____

Vehicles.. $_____

Deprecitation Schedule:

Office equipment (years) .... _____

Vehicles (years) .... _____

Warehouse equipment (years) .... _____

Cash Flow Assumptions:

Prior Accounts Receivable Collected .... _____%

Monthly Sales Collected:

% Collected 0-30 days....................................... _____%

% Collected 31-60 days .... _____%

% Collected 61-90 days .... _____%

% Collected 90+ days .... _____%

Total Monthly Sales Collected .... _____%

Prior Accounts Payable Paid .... _____%

Monthly Expenses Paid:

% Paid 0-30 days .... _____%

% Paid 31-60 days... _____%

% Paid 61-90 days... _____%

% Paid 90+ days .... _____%

Total Monthly Expenses Paid .... _____%

Current Percent of Payroll Paid................................. _____%

Line of Credit:

Annual line of credit interest rate .... _____%

Maximum line of credit...................................... $_____

Notes Payable:

Annual note interest rate .... _____%

Term of note in months..................................... _____

Minimum Cash Balance .... $_____

Additional Funding:

New equity... $_____

New debt (notes payable)................................... $_____

Projected Breakeven Assumptions:

Variable Portion of Cost of Goods .... _____%

Variable Portion of Sales Salaries .... _____%

Variable Portion of Distribution Salary .... _____%

Variable Portion of Administrative Salary .... _____%

Variable Portion of Advertising & Promo .... _____%

Variable Portion of Catalog .... _____%

Variable Portion of Travel.................................... _____%

Assumption Statement
General Purpose

	Data Input
Revenue Forecast Assumptions:	
Annual Revenue Amount	$_____
Increase In Revenues Per Year	_____%
Income Statement Assumptions:	
Cost Of Sales: (choose 1, below)	
Percent of sales, or	_____%
Dollar amount per year	$_____
Annual Salaries and Wages:	
Salaries	$_____
Payroll tax and benefit rate	_____%
Annual Occupancy Expense:	
Rent	$_____
Insurance	$_____
Repairs and maintenance	$_____
Utilities	$_____
Annual Operating Expenses:	
Advertising and promotion	$_____
Office expense	$_____
Professional fees	$_____
Stationery and printing	$_____
Telephone	$_____
Other 1	$_____
Other 2	$_____
Other 3	$_____
Balance Sheet Assumptions:	
Property and Equipment Purchased:	
Office equipment	$_____
Depreciation Schedule:	
Office equipment (years)	_____
Cash Flow Assumptions:	
Prior Accounts Receivable Collected	_____%
Annual Revenues Collected:	
% Collected 0 — 30 days	_____%
% Collected 31 — 60 days	_____%
% Collected 61 — 90 days	_____%
% Collected 90+ days	_____%
Total Annual Revenues Collected	_____%
Prior Accounts Payable Paid	_____%
Annual Expenses Paid:	
% Paid 0 — 30 days	_____%
% Paid 31 — 60 days	_____%
% Paid 61 — 90 days	_____%
% Paid 90+ days	_____%
Total Annual Expenses Paid	_____%
Notes Payable:	
Annual note interest rate	_____%
Term of note in months	_____
Minimum Cash Balance	$_____

Additional Funding:
    New equity .... $_____
    New debt (notes payable) .... $_____

Projected Breakeven Assumptions:
    Variable Portion Of Cost Of Sales .... _____%
    Variable Portion Of Salaries and Wages .... _____%
    Variable Portion Of Operating Expenses .... _____%

Assumption Statement
Personal

Income Assumptions: <u>Data Input</u>

Total Annual Gross Salaries, Commissions . . . . $_____

Performance And Merit Increase Rate. . . . . _____%

Bonuses. . . . . $_____

Federal & State Payroll Withholding Rate . . . . _____%

Other Income . . . . $_____

Annual Interest Rate On Cash Accounts. . . . . _____%

Annual Dividend Rate On Stocks & Mutuals . . . . _____%

Annual Interest Rate On Tax-Exempt Bonds . . . . _____%

Annual Interest Rate On Corporate Bonds. . . . . _____%

Expense Assumptions:

Monthly Housing Costs:

Monthly rent payment . . . . $_____

Monthly mortgage principle and interest. . . . . $_____

Annual mortgage interest rate . . . . _____%

Number of months left on mortgage . . . . _____

Real estate tax assumptions:

Annual real estate taxes . . . . $_____

Are your taxes collected monthly by a lending institution?
(Enter 1 if YES, or 0 if NO). _____

If you answered NO, in which month are
your real estate taxes due?:

Month of your first tax payment . . . . _____

Number of months between payments. . . . . _____

Home casualty insurance. . . . . $_____

Lawn, pool, snow, rubbish services . . . . $_____

Repairs and maintenance. . . . . $_____

Utilities (heat, light, and water). . . . . $_____

Telephone . . . . $_____

Monthly Automobile Costs:

Automobile insurance. . . . . $_____

Automobile licenses and excise tax . . . . $_____

Gas and oil . . . . $_____

Maintenance and repairs . . . . $_____

Automobile #1 loan payment. . . . . $_____

Automobile #1 loan interest rate . . . . _____%

Automobile #2 purchase price. . . . . $_____

Automobile #2 to be purchased in what month . . . . _____

Automobile #2 loan amount. . . . . $_____

Automobile #2 loan interest rate . . . . _____%

Number of months financed on loan . . . . _____

Automobile lease payment. . . . . $_____

Monthly Insurance And Medical Costs:

Dentist and orthodontist . . . . $_____

Doctors and hospitals. . . . . $_____

Insurance, disability . . . . $_____

Insurance, term life . . . . $_____

Insurance, medical and dental. . . . . $_____

Monthly Educational Expense:

Children's education . . . . $_____

Professional education . . . . $_____
Evening courses . . . . $_____
Monthly Food Costs:
    Groceries . . . . $_____
    Restaurants . . . . $_____
Monthly Alimony/Child Support:
    Alimony . . . . $_____
    Child support . . . . $_____
Monthly Discretionary And Other:
    Charitable donations . . . . $_____
    Clothing . . . . $_____
    Gifts . . . . $_____
    Memberships and subscriptions . . . . $_____
    Other discretionary . . . . $_____
    Pets . . . . $_____
    Vacations . . . . $_____

Balance Sheet Assumptions:
Purchase of New Residence:
    Purchase price of new residence . . . . $_____
    Total closing costs incurred . . . . $_____
    Month of purchase (closing month) . . . .   _____
    Mortgage loan amount . . . . $_____
    Annual interest rate of mortgage . . . .   _____%
    Term of mortgage in months . . . .   _____
Sale of Current Residence:
    Selling price of current residence . . . . $_____
    Selling expenses incurred . . . . $_____
    Original cost plus improvements . . . . $_____
    Month of sale (closing month) . . . .   _____
Purchase Of Other Assets:
    Jewelry and collectibles . . . . $_____
    Furniture and appliances . . . . $_____
    Major home improvements . . . . $_____

Net Worth Assumptions:
Annual Appreciation Rate:
    Single premium life annuity . . . .   _____%
    Jewelry and collectibles . . . .   _____%
    Residence . . . .   _____%
    Retirement plan(s) . . . .   _____%

Cash Flow Assumptions:
Refinancing Of Current Residence:
    Refinanced amount . . . . $_____
    Refinancing closing costs . . . . $_____
    Month of refinancing . . . .   _____
    Refinanced mortgage interest rate . . . .   _____%
    Number of months refinanced . . . .   _____
Home Owners Equity Loan:
    Amount borrowed . . . . $_____
    Amount repaid . . . . $_____
    Annual equity loan interest rate . . . .   _____%
Bank Line Of Credit:
    Line of credit borrowings . . . . $_____
    Line of credit repayments . . . . $_____

Annual line of credit interest rate . . . . _____%

Federal And State Income Taxes:
    If you make estimated tax payments,
    enter your quarterly tax payment amount . . . . $_____
    Enter any tax refunds (payments) due . . . . $_____
    Federal and state income tax rate . . . . _____%

Notes Receivable:
    Notes receivable lendings . . . . $_____
    Notes receivable collections . . . . $_____
    Note receivable annual interest rate . . . . _____%

Credit Card Charge Accounts:
    Percent of monthly expenses charged:
        Housing—furniture and appliances . . . . _____%
        Housing—repairs and maintenance . . . . _____%
        Automobile—gas and oil . . . . _____%
        Automobile—maintenance and repairs . . . . _____%
        Total insurance and medical . . . . _____%
        Food—restaurants . . . . _____%
        Total discretionary and other . . . . _____%
    Monthly charge card dollar amount paid . . . . $_____

Investment Portfolio Assumptions:
    Stock #1:
        Number of stock #1 shares purchased . . . . _____
        Stock #1's per share purchase price . . . . $_____
        Number of stock #1 shares sold . . . . _____
        Stock #1's per share selling price . . . . $_____
        Annual appreciation of stock #1 . . . . _____%
        Brokerage fee rate for stock #1 . . . . _____%
    Stock #2:
        Number of stock #2 shares purchased . . . . _____
        Stock #2's per share purchase price . . . . $_____
        Number of stock #2 shares sold . . . . _____
        Stock #2's per share selling price . . . . $_____
        Annual appreciation of stock #2 . . . . _____%
        Brokerage fee rate for stock #2 . . . . _____%
    Mutual Fund:
        Number of mutual fund shares purchased . . . . _____
        Mutual fund's per share purchase price . . . . $_____
        Number of mutual fund shares sold . . . . _____
        Mutual fund's per share selling price . . . . $_____
        Annual appreciation of mutual fund . . . . _____%
    Tax-Exempt Municipal Bond:
        Number of tax-exempt shares purchased . . . . _____
        Tax-exempt's per share purchase price . . . . $_____
        Number of tax-exempt shares sold . . . . _____
        Tax-exempt's per share selling price . . . . $_____
        Annual appreciation of tax-exempt bond . . . . _____%
    Retirement Fund:
        Retirement contributions . . . . $_____
        Retirement withdrawals . . . . $_____
    Single Premium Annuity:
        Single premium annuity payment . . . . $_____
        Single premium loan borrowings . . . . $_____
        Single premium loan repayments . . . . $_____

Single premium loan interest rate . . . .   _____%

Corporate Bonds:
 Corporate bonds purchased . . . .   \$_____
 Corporate bonds sold . . . .   \$_____

Preparing Financial Projections Manually

I n order to answer the five key financial questions, you must develop three types of financial projections for each alternative venture concept under consideration. The three types of projections (or proforma analyses) are:

1. Profit and Loss (P&L) Projection

2. Balance Sheet Projection; and,

3. Cash Flow Projection.

In addition, you will want to prepare a personal financial statement to better assess your own ability to fund your venture, and to show to outside investors/lenders as part of your funding proposal. Any assumptions made in estimating the numbers should be footnoted and summarized on a separate page after each appropriate financial statement.

You can generate a projected profit and loss statement with nothing more than an estimate of future sales and expenses. Certain expenses may increase in proportion to sales increases and should be projected as such. If you have additional information about future production, sales, and overhead charges, you will be better able to project revenues or losses.

The proforma balance sheet statement lists all of your venture's assets, liabilities, and equities. Enter the appropriate figures as forecasted for the period. This forecast will show you whether your venture has the resources it needs to meet its sales objectives.

Having enough cash on hand to pay all disbursements is essential if your venture is to survive. The proforma cash flow indicates whether your venture will have sufficient cash for the coming year or whether you will need outside funding. You should fill out the cash flow on a monthly basis so that you can determine the maximum cash required during the period and when that maximum cash need will occur.

WARNING: If you are preparing these projections with a calculator or spreadsheet, you must understand that the individual statements are not integrated and consequently may contain inaccurate numbers upon which you may (unknowingly) be basing important decisions. You will also find it tedious, if not impossible, to produce multiple sets of projections needed to compare different venture alternatives.

You are able to make better decisions if you produce these financial projections with the assistance of Ronstadt's FINANCIALS.

Projected Profit & Loss Statement

Year Ending _____

Revenue
  Gross Sales $ _____
    Less Returns & Allowances   _____
  Net Sales   _____

  Cost of Sales   _____

  Gross Profit   _____

Operating Expenses   _____

Selling
    Salaries and Wages   _____
    Payroll Taxes   _____
    Commissions   _____
    Advertising   _____
    Other   _____
Total Selling Expenses $ _____

  General & Administrative   _____
    Salaries & Wages   _____
    Payroll Taxes   _____
    Employee Benefits   _____
    Insurance   _____
    Depreciation   _____
    Automobile Expense   _____
    Dues & Subscriptions   _____
    Legal & Accounting   _____
    Office Supplies   _____
    Telephone   _____
    Utilities   _____
    Rent   _____
    Taxes & Licenses   _____
    Other   _____

  Total General & Administrative $ _____

Total Operating Expenses $ _____

Operating Profit (Loss)   _____

Other Income and Expenses   _____

Net Income (Loss) Before Taxes $ _____

  Income Taxes   _____

Net Income (Loss) $ _____

Proforma Balance Sheet

Period Ending _____

Assets
   Current Assets:
      Cash and Equivalents $ _____
      Accounts Receivable, net of allowance for bad debts   _____
      Inventories   _____
      Prepaid Expenses   _____
        Total Current Assets   _____

   Fixed Assets:
      Land   _____
      Buildings   _____
      Equipment   _____
      Furniture   _____
      Vehicles   _____
      Less: Accumulated Depreciation   _____
        Total Fixed Assets, Net   _____

   Other Assets   _____

Total Assets $ _____

Liabilities and Shareholders' Equity
   Current Liabilities
      Accounts Payable $ _____
      Short-Term Debt   _____
      Current Portion of Long-Term Debt   _____
      Income Taxes Payable   _____
      Accrued Expenses   _____
        Total Current Liabilities   _____

   Long Term Debt   _____

      Shareholders' Equity   _____
      Capital Stock   _____
      Additional Paid-In Capital   _____
      Retained Earnings (Deficit)   _____
        Total Shareholders' Equity   _____

Total Liabilities and Shareholders' Equity $ _____

Proforma Cash Flow

Period Starting _____ **Ending** _____

	Month 1	Month 2
Beginning Cash Balance	$ _____	$ _____
Cash Receipts		
Cash Sales	_____	_____
Accounts Receivable Collections	_____	_____
Other	_____	_____
Total Cash Receipts	$ _____	$ _____
Cash Disbursements		
Inventory Purchases	_____	_____
Salaries and Wages	_____	_____
Fixed Assets	_____	_____
Rent	_____	_____
Insurance	_____	_____
Utilities	_____	_____
Interest	_____	_____
Advertising	_____	_____
Taxes	_____	_____
Other Payments	_____	_____
Total Cash Disbursed	$ _____	$ _____
Total Operating Cash Surplus (Deficit)	$ _____	$ _____
Additional Funding (Repayments)	$ _____	$ _____
Ending Cash Balance	$ _____	$ _____

Personal Financial Statement

Period Ending _____

Assets

Cash	$ _____
Savings Accounts	_____
Stocks, Bonds, Other securities	_____
Accounts/Notes Receivable	_____
Life Insurance Cash Value	_____
Rebates/Refunds	_____
Autos/Other Vehicles	_____
Real Estate	_____
Vested Pension Plan/Retirement Accounts	_____
Other Assets	_____
Total Assets	$ _____

Liabilities

Student Loans	_____
Credit Card Balance Payable	_____
Notes Payable	_____
Automobile Loans	_____
Taxes Payable	_____
Real Estate Loans	_____
Other Liabilities	_____
Total Liabilities	$ _____
Net Worth	$ _____
Total Liabilities and Net Worth	$ _____

Glossary

The following words and phrases are frequently used business terms. Most of them are found throughout this guide and are highlighted in CAPITAL LETTERS in the text of the various modules. The definitions are our own. The context in which we use them may not necessarily be the same context in which other sources use them.

ADMINISTRATIVE SYSTEMS — internal procedures for handling bookkeeping functions, such as accounts receivable, accounts payable, checking/investment accounts, payroll and other financial and office functions.

ADVERTISING ALLOWANCES — an arrangement with a supplier, customer, distributor, retailer or other party to advertise or promote your product in exchange for a reduced rate or higher margins for themselves.

ADVERTISING MEDIUMS — trade journals, newspapers, magazines, radio, T.V. and other forms of communication that reaches your customers.

ASSUMPTIONS — preconceived notions or hunches on which you base reasonable financial projections or other probable developments.

BACK-UP SYSTEM — procedure and contingency plans for switching to other available equipment should your main equipment breakdown or become unusable. Switching to other available suppliers should your primary suppliers go out of business or stop servicing you.

BENEFICIAL IMPACTS — the positive results your product will have on customers, the community, economy, environment or other societal force. The problem it solves, the opportunity it fulfills, the needs it meets.

BRAINSTORMING — a management technique used to foster ideas, solve problems, set goals, establish priorities and make assignments for their accomplishment.

BREAK-EVEN POINT — the point at which all fixed and variable costs associated with manufacturing a product and doing business equals the amount of income from sales.

COMMON STOCK — documents that represent the book value of the business. Also known as capital stock, common stock certifies the amount of ownership in the company.

LORD PUBLISHING, INC., 1988

COMPENSATION PACKAGE — the total value a founder, manager, or other employee receives for their involvement in the business. May include salary, share of profits, stock or other type of ownership and other benefits (insurance, auto, retirement plan, etc.).

CONSIGNMENT SALES — having a retailer, wholesaler or other sales outlet obtain and stock your product at no charge, and taking a predetermined percent of the gross receipts when they sell it.

CONVERTIBLE DEBENTURES — a loan that allows the debt holder to choose whether or not to convert the remaining outstanding debt into stock at a predetermined price.

CORPORATE AFFILIATIONS — the position, role, or association a member of your Board of Directors or management team has with other companies. (Important to show experience, contacts or possible conflict of interests.)

COPYRIGHT — legal protection that prevents any party from duplication or using any material or information from a publication without expressed approval from the owners of the publication.

CYCLE ORDER — as it applies to an inventory control system; a procedure for ordering or replacing stock based on predictable levels of activity with production or within the industry (seasonal factors).

DEBT WITH WARRANTS — a loan that obligates the company to repay a certain amount of money over a certain period of time at an agreed upon rate, carrying with it the right to purchase stock at a fixed price within a specified period of time. (Differs from convertible debentures in that all debts must be repaid and, in addition, the note holder is given warrants. Under convertible debentures, the note holder might not recoup the full loan before buying the stock.)

DEMOGRAPHICS — a profile of the measurable distinctions of a target market, including: age, sex, marital status, family size, income, profession, education level, etc.

DIRECT MARKET — the easiest, fastest and least expensive area or contact with the company's target market for product introduction.

DISTINCTIVE COMPETENCE — the training, skills, talents, education, experience and performance an individual or company possesses. Whatever it is that you do well, makes you special from most others.

DISTRIBUTION NETWORK (or CHANNELS) — the method used to get the product from manufacturing to the consumer. Common distributors are wholesalers, retailers and manufacturer's representatives.

DOWNTIME — the periods or amount of time that equipment or operations stop running, due to service maintenance, repairs, breakage or lack of business.

EARNING PROJECTIONS — the amount of revenue a business expects to receive from sales, investment or other income producing operations within a given period. Usually displayed on an income (profit and loss) statement and/or cash flow statement. See proformas.

ECONOMIC BENEFITS (Trickle Down Effect) — the positive results your company has on the economy, i.e., creating jobs, injection of new capital into the community, increasing the revenues of existing businesses, etc.

EFFICIENCY RATIOS (Conversion Rates) — as it applies to marketing a product/service the amount of time, calls, money, ads, mailing and other marketing activities it takes to make a sale. Example: 50 calls to get 10 presentations. Ten presentations to get one sale.

FIXED ORDER — as it applies to an inventory control system; a procedure for ordering or replacing a set amount of stock at a predetermined time (every three months).

FIXED vs. VARIABLE COSTS — fixed costs DO NOT vary with the level of output, i.e., salaries and rent. Variable costs vary with the level of output, i.e., supplies and overtime.

GROWTH PATTERNS — the trends and positive speculations within an industry that indicates a promising outlook for business. Growth patters are based on the overall economic condition, emerging technology, effect of government regulation (or deregulation) and other indicators.

GROWTH POTENTIAL — the increased amount of money, expansion, activity and other developments that are likely for a company based upon the popularity and marketing of its product/service, management skills, industry growth patterns and other factors.

INDUSTRY PROFILE — the history, participants, total sales volume, trends, growth potential and other pertinent facts on a particular industry.

INDUSTRY STANDARD — a common basis of operating, pay levels, etc. between companies in the same industry. Example: it is now an industry standard for fast food restaurants to have drive-through windows.

INVENTORY CONTROL SYSTEM — a procedure for ordering, replacing and accounting for required. See fixed order and cycle order.

JURISDICTION — the agency or governing body that has the authority to impose and/or enforce regulations.

LEARNING/EXPERIENCE CURVE — expecting performance and results to improve as one gains knowledge and experience. A person's output will be directly proportionate to how much they know about the product, the company, the players and the industry as a whole.

LETTER OF INTENT — a letter addressed to your company from a customer, supplier, distributor or other interested party, stating their desire to do business with you. (A letter of intent does not necessarily oblige the party writing it, but can be an influential device to sway prospective investors to finance the venture based on evident industry and market support).

LEVELS OF (MARKET) PENETRATION — how much of the market you expect to reach. Reaching 10 percent of a nationwide market is a higher level of penetration than reaching 60 percent of a local market. The percent of the market you hope to capture must be specifically defined. The higher the percent, the more resources it will take to reach and service.

LICENSING AGREEMENT — a contractual relationship with a manufacturer and/or distributor to produce and/or sell your product (usually in exchange for royalties).

MBO (MANAGEMENT BY OBJECTIVES) — a management technique for setting goals and objectives, and basing incentives upon their attainment.

MARKET IDENTITY — the ability to create familiarity and loyalty for your product/company in the eyes of the customer through promotions, packaging, labeling, product name and other factors.

MARKET FORCES (BARRIERS) — ingredients in the market that will affect the success of your produce/company, i.e., government regulation, competition, availability of suppliers, etc.

MARKET NICHE — a particular appeal, identity or place in the market that your product/company has. What you do well, different or better than others in the market.

MARKET SEGMENTS — a separation of markets by broad categories, i.e., by product, by customer, by geography, by industry. Example: marketing computers for the home is a segment different from marketing computers to businesses.

MARKET SHARE — the percent of the target market a company hopes to capture.

MARKET TRENDS — factors that indicate where the market is headed, i.e., changes in customer needs or habits, shifts in population, establishment of new industries in the area, etc.

METHODS AND PROCESSES — the technology, operating, assembly or other features that make the product viable and special.

MILESTONES — significant accomplishments attained in the venture, or major junctures the business is steering towards (prototype completion, signing a major customer, etc.).

NONCOMPETE/NONDISCLOSURE AGREEMENTS — legal agreement(s) stipulating that the signee not disclose confidential information about the company and product, and/or preventing the signee from joining or starting a similar venture.

OPERATING ADVANTAGES — the strengths of the business, especially as they apply to the competition. Maybe better equipment, faster production, cheaper transportation and other factors that enhance the efficiency and marketability of the company.

OPERATING COSTS — all expenses involved in running the business. See fixed costs and variable costs.

OPERATING LAYOUT — how the production facilities will be set up. How equipment will be grouped, work stations located, storage, tool shop and other divisions established.

OWNERSHIP INTEREST/DISTRIBUTION — who owns what and how much, i.e., partnership percentage, share of profits kind of stock and number of shares.

PATENT/PATENT PENDING — a grant by the federal government to an inventor of the right to exclude others for a limited time from making, using or selling his invention in this country. A patent may protect the concept, process and/or product itself.

PAYBACK PERIOD — the period of time in which an investor in a start-up can recover initial investment and earn a return on the investment. Most payback periods are between 3–5 years.

LORD PUBLISHING, INC., 1988

PERSONAL FINANCIAL STATEMENTS — assets and liabilities balance sheet and tax returns for three years. (Sometimes required by prospective investors of the founders/managers of the start-up.)

PREFERRED STOCK — stock granting guaranteed dividends or other rights above that of common stock.

PRIMARY SUPPLIERS — the critical major suppliers of parts, components and other goods and services to your company, upon which your business depends.

PRINCIPALS (KEY PEOPLE) — the founders, managers, Board of Directors and other important decision makers of a start-up company.

PRODUCT APPLICATIONS — the potential uses of your product, perhaps directed at different markets.

PRODUCTION CAPACITY — the total amount of equipment, space, time or other resources available to achieve maximum output.

PRODUCTIVITY QUOTAS — the amount of salary, commissions, bonuses or other payments based on specific levels of production and performance.

PROFIT POTENTIAL — the amount of money, less cost of goods sold, that can be make from a product in a particular industry based on predetermined levels of production and set prices.

PROFORMAS — projected financial performance statements include: balance sheet, income sheet and cash flow sheet.

PROTOTYPE — a model, mockup or first assembly of a new product.

PROXIMITY TO CUSTOMER BASE — geographical location of a company's target market in relation to the company. Mode of marketing, delivery and service is considered.

QUALITY CONTROL SYSTEM — procedures, checks and balances used to ensure the integrity of each product unit.

REGULATORY (APPROVAL) REQUIREMENTS — the restrictions, licenses, laws and regulations applicable to a product or company, imposed by federal, state or local government agencies.

RIGHTS AND OPTIONS — as it applies to investment in a start-up; the agreement outlining what, how and when ownership and payback is exercised.

ROI (RETURN ON INVESTMENT) — the annual percent or money made from investing in a start-up over a specified period of time.

STAGE OF DEVELOPMENT — as it applies to a product; prototype, research and development, short-run production, full production (distribution or other level of activity). As it applies to a company; start-up, expansion/diversification or other level of operation. As it applies to an industry; introduction, growth, maturity, peak/saturation, decline.

STRAIGHT DEBT — a form of financing a start-up. A loan at a specific interest rate to be repaid over a set number of months.

TARGET MARKET — particular segment(s) of the market which the product is directed towards. The initial customers you hope to win over.

TAX BENEFITS — the deductions, protection, savings and other shelters that result from investing in a start-up.

TRADEMARK — protection of a company's name, logo or other symbol, by the U.S. Government, preventing another party from using it.

WORKFLOW/PRODUCTION CONTROL PROCEDURES — the best use of equipment, personnel, supplies, materials and other resources to maintain efficient operations.

LORD PUBLISHING, INC., 1988

References

1. McLaughlin, Harold J., *Building Your Business Plan*, John Wiley & Sons, 1985.

2. Mancuso, Joseph R., *How to Prepare and Present a Business Plan*, Prentice-Hall, Inc. Englewood Cliffs, New Jersey, 1983.

3. Mancuso, Joseph R., *How to Write a Winning Business Plan*, Prentice-Hall, Inc., Englewood Cliffs, New Jersey, 1985.

4. White, Richard M. Jr., *The Entrepreneur's Manual*, Chilton Book Company, Radnor, Pennsylvania, 1977.

5. Howell, Robert A., *How to Write a Business Plan*, American Management Association, 1982.

6. Butler, Robert E. and Rappaport, Donald, *Describing Your Business — An Important Part of Financing*, Price Waterhouse, New York, New York.

7. A Guide to Preparation of a Business Plan, *The Fundamentals of Structuring and Pricing a Venture Financing*, Peat Marwick, Minneapolis, Minnesota.

8. *Manufacturing Business Plan*, Small Business Management Systems, Manitoba, Canada.

9. Block, Zenas and MacMillan, Ian C., "Milestones for Successful Venture Planning, Growing Concerns," Harvard Business Review, Cambridge, Massachusetts, September–October, 1985.

10. Osgood, William R., Dr., *Business Plan Format*, South Dakota Business Development Centers.

11. *Outline for a New Venture Business Plan*, Arthur Young, 1984.

12. Ronstadt, Robert, *Entrepreneurial Finance — Taking Control of Your Financial Decision Making*, Lord Publishing, Inc., Natick, MA, 1988.

13. Ronstadt, Robert and Shuman, Jeffrey, *Venture Feasibility Planning Guide*, Lord Publishing, Inc., Natick, MA, 1988.

Evaluation

Receive Free: **"Networking for Success: Know-Who Plus Know-How"**
Just return the following evaluation to receive your FREE copy. Your
feedback will help us to improve the book.

1. Where did your hear about *The Business Plan?*
   ☐ Recommended by a friend/consultant
   ☐ Magazine/newspaper article (which one) _____
   ☐ Received direct mail invitation
   ☐ Other _____

2. Why did you decide to order/use the planning guide?
   ☐ To see if my idea was feasible
   ☐ To write a comprehensive business plan
   ☐ As a gift (resource) for someone else
   ☐ Other _____

3. Did you write a business plan using the book as a guide?
   ☐ Yes   ☐ No
   If yes, did you find it:
   ☐ Easy to use — a great help
   ☐ Somewhat easy to use — helpful
   ☐ Difficult to use — not very helpful

4. Did you use (or intend to use) the book to write a plan for:
   ☐ Ongoing management and planning of a venture
   ☐ Funding sources — to raise money
   ☐ Other _____

5. What sections of the planning guide were most valuable to you?
   _____
   _____

6. What sections of the planning guide were least valuable to you?
   _____
   _____

7. What changes would you make in format or content?
   _____
   _____

8. Did the book help you to launch a venture or accomplish another
   goal?   ☐ Yes   ☐ No
   If yes, the name of the company started or goal accomplished
   _____

9. Would you recommend *The Business Plan* to others? Why or why not?
   _____
   _____

Note: Don't forget to include your return address on the back side so we
can send you **"Networking for Success: Know-Who Plus Know-How."**

L O R D   P U B L I S H I N G ,   I N C . ,   1 9 8 8

---------------------------------- Fold Here ------------------------------------

---------------------------------- Fold Here ------------------------------------

From _____

_____

_____

Lord Publishing, Inc.

P.O. Box 806

Dover, MA 02030

Staple Here